The Tales Of Dod

by

Grahame Howard

This book is dedicated to the Woog
(20.5.1948 to 1.8.2007)
and to our parents the Dod and the Zomp,
without whom this book would not have been possible.

First published in 2010 by
The Bellfield Press,
4 Bellfield Terrace, Edinburgh, EH15 2BJ
www.gkbenterprises.fsnet.co.uk

Copyright Graham Howard 2010

A CIP record for this book is available form the British Library

ISBN 9780 9526554 9 7   Price £4.50

Printed by McKenzie Quality Print, Kirkhill, Dyce, AB21 0GN

CONTENTS

CHAPTER 1: THE MAKING OF DOD

We were living in Norwich, and I would be about eight, when Peter, my elder brother by five years, came home from school one day, walked into the kitchen of No. 3 Constitution Hill and announced to the rest of the family – who had gathered there to make the most of the warmth of the Aga – that henceforth he was to be called the Woog. In addition I was to be the Spoz, and our mother the Zomp. Finally, he announced that our father was to be the Dod. In later years this sort of behaviour would have been attributed, quite reasonably, to a longer than usual session in the Constitution, a nearby hostelry. It is true that for generations the Howards had been prodigious drinkers from an early age but at thirteen years old, on this occasion, this was not the case. It is a testimony to the Woog's perseverance that those names have stuck to this day.

My mother and father found these new names quite hard to get to grips with. Having baptised us Peter Neville, and Grahame Charles William, and they themselves being called Bill and Shirley for all their lives thus far, they understandably found the transition quite difficult. My mother in particular would often get the names mixed up, and in moments of emotion would shout, 'Oh, Dodspozwoog!', a sort of collective name for anyone who might have perpetrated some minor misdemeanour, usually flatulence. One might think that this name-changing represented one of those phases that psychologists talk about, like having a phantom friend. Not so. This new baptism was to last for the rest of our lives, and to this day when in the Woog's company, if someone calls him Peter, I look around to see whom they are addressing.

I have no idea if this identity realignment bore a causal relationship to some of Dod's slightly bizarre behaviour. I suspect not, as there were early signs of eccentricity which predated the new name, but it could hardly have helped. The Dod should have been an Edwardian man of leisure. Work did not suit him and in fairness he was not very good at it, but sadly an income was necessary. Brought up in an age where middle-class families had a maid or two, a gardener and people who 'did' for them, he managed the changing social circumstances of the twentieth century very badly: in fact he never managed them at all.

In his previous incarnation as William Titchmarsh Howard he had had a number of jobs, the most enduring of which was with the Norwich Union, initially in London. This was ideal for him as it involved an enormous amount of beer drinking, and to be a successful insurance underwriter a voracious thirst was essential.

Dod frequently said, 'No one ever got any business by staying in the office', and he didn't – either stay in the office or get business. I suspect the current crop of trendy London businessmen might call this networking. Dod networked hard and long, and networked a lot with his immediate senior, Frank Crabbe. Crabby, as Dod called him, was highly trained and endowed with an enormous thirst, so that after an hour or two in his city office it would be off to Fleet Street to do a ten-pint lunchtime network. It was then back to the office to check that everything was all right, and back out networking by five-thirty. This was cutting-edge stuff, and for Dod a tough but sound grounding in the insurance business. Following a few years of this intensive apprenticeship he was deemed adequately trained to be moved to Head Office in Norwich. After a brief spell in a rented flat at Albermarle House where the gardener taught me how to make a bow and arrow from sticks and a piece of string – a skill which to date has proved to be of no use to me whatsoever – we moved into No. 3 Constitution Hill, on the north side of the city. No. 3 was a red brick, semi-detached Edwardian house with a large white pyramid-shaped gable and a mock half-timbered appearance to the front. Between the house and the pavement was a low brick wall which bore the inevitable stumps of the iron railings which had been removed during the Second World War. The front garden was an Edwardian delicacy with a rectangular pattern of raised borders and a path around a small pond in the middle. A porch with waist-high wooden railings surrounded the large, impressive black-painted front door. The house had four bedrooms, excellent access to the No. 89 bus (whose terminus was at the back of the house on Wall Road) and a long garden, at the end of which was an air-raid shelter with trees growing out of it. In the years to come this would make an excellent Spanish galleon or Sopwith Camel, depending upon which game I was playing. Moreover No. 3 was about one hundred and fifty yards from a public house called the Constitution Tavern.

CHAPTER 2: No. 3 CONSTITUTION HILL

The electric frying pan was probably the most unusual thing we found in the loft of our new house. More mundane items from on an earlier inspection were a bayonet from the First World War, a belt of live ammunition, and a very fine doll's house.

I have never, before or since, seen an electric frying pan like this one. It had a diameter of about twelve inches, was enormously heavy and under the impressive iron pan there was a naked electric coil which glowed red when it was plugged in and switched on. The electric coil was completely unprotected, so that a less than careful operator could quite easily receive a burn and an electric shock simultaneously. I think we did on occasions use the pan for frying, but it was a much more versatile instrument than that.

No. 3 Constitution Hill had no central heating. In fact it had no heating at all, apart from the coke-fired Aga in the kitchen and open coal fires in the two main downstairs rooms. As the Aga was our only means of cooking, it had to remain alight all year round. This meant that the whole house was tropical in the summer but in the winter only the kitchen temperature was above freezing. Norfolk is cold, with north-easterly winds blowing straight from Siberia and nothing to stop them until they entered No. 3 through its ill-fitting windows and doors. It was cold. It was very cold! In winter we had ice patterns on the inside of the bedroom windows. But if there was one room colder than the others, it was the back toilet. This was not strictly an outside toilet as it was attached to the main structure of the house but it was only protected on one side by a rather flimsy conservatory.

Woog and I discovered early on that it was unwise to use the downstairs toilet in winter since it was likely to become completely frozen and was akin to going to the toilet in the middle of the Arctic tundra. If you went for a piss, the urine would simply cover the thick layer of ice which filled the pan, momentarily melting the uppermost layer, only to become part of this ice plug within a few minutes. There seemed to be no easy solution to this; candles didn't help and just added the risk of a burn to that of frostbite for those who used the closet. Sitting down in this toilet was particularly ill-advised – not only was hypothermia a real possibility but the wooden seat had a crack in it. The mechanics of this were such that, as the weight of one's buttocks hit the seat, the crack closed, thereby pinching the portion of buttock applied and resulting in a painful and potentially serious injury. Cruelly, when we were older, Woog and I thought it a huge wheeze to direct girlfriends to this toilet and then wait to hear the resulting squeals. Clearly some heating was required. They say that necessity is the mother of invention and Dod came up with a plan so simple, yet so brilliant.

'You know what, dear?' he said to Zomp after unsuccessfully trying to unfreeze the toilet one cold Sunday. 'I think I'll put that electric frying pan in the toilet to heat it up a bit.'

'Are you sure that's safe?' she replied. There was no answer. Dod was already on the case.

Half an hour later the job was complete. Using a few pieces of string, Dod had suspended the pan (of the electric variety) from the ceiling above the pan (of the toilet variety).

'There you are, dear,' Dod said triumphantly, as the ice melted and the toilet flushed.

'Are you sure that's safe?' repeated Zomp as she surveyed Dod's handiwork.

'Of course it is!' Dod never lacked confidence in his Heath Robinson creations.

This was wizard. With the frying pan hanging in the toilet, not only did the toilet flush – that is if you used the secret technique, which was two quick tugs and one long pull on the chain and if that failed, two longs usually did the trick – but, with care not to leave the door open, the back toilet became the warmest room in the house, and if it had been a bit larger we would have entertained in there.

There was a similar problem in the loft where the cold-water tank would regularly ice over. Once again the frying pan came to the rescue, this time suspended by pieces of string from a rafter above the tank. The water tank had no lid on it and if one of Dod's knots had failed and the live frying pan had descended into the cold-water tank, we would probably have plunged the whole of North Norwich into darkness. Once again, however, Dod had complete confidence in his system, seemed to think it quite safe, and it worked.

Thus in the winter months the frying pan alternated between the back toilet and the loft. After a period spent in the toilet Dod would observe to Zomp, 'The toilet's flushing nicely now, dear. I'll just pop the pan in the loft for a while.'

'Do be careful, dear', Zomp would reply as she watched with trepidation while Dod ascended into the loft with the live, glowing frying pan in one hand and a selection of pieces of string of varying lengths in the other.

Dod spent a considerable amount of time getting in and out of the loft. Once the live ammunition and the bayonet (which had a brown stain on the webbing which the Woog said was blood – human blood), had found their way into the toy cupboard, Dod found that the loft was also home to a television aerial. Dod said it was a special type called an internal aerial. In fact it was nothing of the sort, being simply an external aerial which had been left lying in the loft. This probably explained the appalling picture, or complete lack of one, when we eventually connected it to a television set.

Whenever we wanted to watch television there was a well-rehearsed routine. About an hour before the programme we wanted to watch was due to start, all of us went into the sitting room where the television was located and Dod switched it on to see if there was a picture. There never was a picture – only a snowstorm accompanied by a crackling sound. But we were optimists. Dod would then twiddle the tuning knob a bit, trying to find that elusive positioning which could give us some indication of where a picture might be located. Ever the optimist, Zompie would sit expectantly in front of the set waiting for the programme to begin.

'What do you think, dear. Any sign of a picture yet?' Dod would ask intermittently.

'Nothing so far,' she'd reply.

'Are you *quite* sure?' Dod would say in a way that somehow implied it was Zompie's fault that there was no picture and that she wasn't looking hard enough.

'There might have been something just then. Go back a bit.' After about fifteen minutes when with luck we had located a ghostly image, Dod would make the ascent into the loft. As there was no ladder, this in itself was a tricky manoeuvre involving a bedside table and two kitchen chairs, which had to be brought upstairs specially for the purpose. With the aerial held in one hand Dod then moved around the loft, stepping from rafter to rafter while waving it about in the hope that ultimately a picture would appear. On the appearance of an image, however faint, the would-be viewer (normally Zomp) would shout loudly, 'Stop!' at the ceiling in the general direction of the loft, at which command Dod would cease his perambulations and, while attempting to hold the aerial stationary, would begin phase two of the procedure.

A more refined technique was to have a third person stationed halfway up the stairs. The first person – normally Woog or Zomp – would stand in the doorway of the sitting room, and on the appearance of a half-decent picture would make a signal to me on the stairs who would then yell to Dod through the open loft hatch. This technique had the disadvantage of having a built-in

7

time delay which could be crucial if Dod was moving around the loft at speed. Once the optimal position had been identified, there was then the difficulty of anchoring the aerial. This second phase would involve numerous bits of string of different lengths, along with a coat hanger or two. Not surprisingly, this rarely worked and often the only way to watch television was to have someone permanently in the loft moving about, as and when necessary, while the rest of the family watched television downstairs.

It was not just the aerial that was a problem. Dod had a legion of friends, one of whom was an electrician who gave us an endless supply of half-broken televisions. At one stage we had two, one set on top of the other. The top one produced the sound and the bottom one the picture, or it might have been the other way about. Anyway it doesn't matter, since after a few weeks of watching this set-up, one of them, either the top or bottom one (I can't remember which) blew up while Woog and I were watching a particularly exciting episode of *Dr Who*. There was a loud bang, following which smoke and then flames erupted from the back of the stack of televisions. Initially we thought that these were very realistic special effects but, when the smoke cleared, the appearance of the burned-out shell of one the sets and the complete absence of the Doctor or the Daleks, confirmed the fact that one of the television sets had indeed exploded.

'Gosh!' I said as I dived behind the settee.

Woog, being five years older than me, had a better command of expletives, and yelled 'Bloody hell!' as he joined me there.

For some time after the unpleasantness of the exploding television we had none at all and then there appeared a pay-as-you-go version which I suspect had something to do with a poor rental payment record. There was a slot for shillings in the back. Once a coin was inserted you turned a key and, lo and behold, a picture appeared. I think three shillings lasted about two hours and when we wanted to watch a programme Dod would put some money in the back.

'That'll be plenty,' he always reassured us.

Knowing this was seldom the case, Zomp liked to have confirmation. 'Are you sure, Bill? You know what happened last time.'

Dod invariably replied in the affirmative and was always nearly, but never completely, correct. The money inevitably ran out near the end and therefore at the climax of the programme. As the picture faded to a small white dot in the middle of the screen, Woog and myself would shout in unison, 'Oh no! Not again!'

'Damn! I'm sure that should have been enough. Must be a longer that usual program; just as it was getting interesting too,' was the inevitable response from Dod.

'Has anyone got a shilling? Has anyone got a shilling?' Woog would shout excitedly, looking at Dod and then at Zomp's sleeping form. Dod had already used up all his coins, so we then shook Zomp – who always fell asleep within a minute or two of sitting down – until she woke up. 'Have you any spare shillings?' we would all ask together. Not surprisingly, Zomp, initially somewhat disorientated and oblivious to the urgency of the situation, would reply vaguely, 'Must have dozed off. What time is it, dear? Just been resting my eyes.' After a moment she would spot the black, blank screen and comprehend the seriousness of situation, 'Has it run out again, dear? Oh Bill, you never put enough money in! I think I might have a shilling in my purse.' We then had to question her about the whereabouts of her purse. Still being half asleep, her response was predictably vague. 'I think it might be in the kitchen, or maybe upstairs.' There was then a mad scramble to find her purse and a shilling or two. Of course when one was eventually found and the picture reappeared, the programme had ended and something boring like the News, or even worse, *Farmers' World*, was on. We tried to keep a supply of shillings handy so that we could watch a whole programme uninterrupted. The problem was that this cash reserve was also used as Dod's emergency beer money, which always took precedence. My friends got into the habit of bringing a supply of shilling coins with them if they wanted to watch anything on the television.

Dod had a myriad of friends. As well as the dodgy electrician, there was his gardening friend, who told him that you shouldn't garden when it was wet, or when it was dry or indeed too windy, too cold or too hot. Then there was his garage friend who said you shouldn't ever wash the car after it had rained, as it scratched the cellulose, whatever that was. Then there was his dentist who said that smoking was good for his teeth, as it covered them in a protective coat of nicotine.

With advice like this Dod had lots of free time. While those less well-informed tidied their gardens or cleaned their cars, Dod could only smoke a lot to protect his teeth. His teeth were probably the best protected in Norwich.

Our Aga needed regular attention or it deliberately went out. Twice a day it had to be raked thoroughly, the hot ashes put into a bucket and placed in the back yard, and coke poured in through a hole in the middle of the hot plate. Every now and again it would go out and this would result in a great deal of bad language from Dod. I think Zomp found the change to Aga cooking quite difficult – as you would if you were used to a normal gas or electric stove. The Aga was very good for slow cooking: in fact the slower the better. A joint of meat could be placed in the lower oven (which was the cooler of the two) and it could take upwards of several days before it was ready, especially if the Aga went out in the middle. Cooking times were therefore measured in days rather than minutes. In later years this slow cooking became very useful as it meant there was no need to rush home from the pub. However late we were, we could always be confident that dinner would not be ready.

The Aga required a ceremony every morning. Dod called this 'Argifying' and it could only be done by himself. It was performed at first light, or at least whenever Dod got up. Dressed in Argifying gear, which was his dressing gown in winter, and underpants in summer, he would stand in the middle of the kitchen, rock to and fro, and make energetic hissing sounds. This was followed by the ritual raking out and the topping up with coke, which carried a significant health risk in the underpants-only season. It was vital that this ceremony should not be interrupted. If one of us happened to go into to the kitchen during the procedure, Dod would spin around, begin cleaning the top of the Aga with a special dirty rag and chant, 'Just argifying, dear; just argifying.' Nothing strange in that!

CHAPTER 3: EDWARDIAN DOD

For a few years life continued quite peacefully at No. 3 Constitution Hill, with Dod stuck in a kind of Edwardian time warp. As a young man Dod had been an elegant man about town. His sartorial heroes were Ivor Novello and Anthony Eden; and he aimed to exude the effortless elegance of an Edwardian gentleman. Tall and slim, he had always taken care of his appearance and dressed stylishly. By the time Woog and I were at school he had silver-grey hair and looked every inch the English aristocrat. Well into the 1960s he continued to wear dark three-piece suits for work, the trousers held up by braces, and separate starched white collars, usually with a bold Regency striped shirt. He blamed the Americans for introducing the attached, soft shirt collar and off-the-peg suits. He bought his clothes at Ridley and Livocks in London Street. This was one of those wonderful old-fashioned gentlemen's outfitters which was more like a club than a shop. The sales staff were nearly all male and knew most of their clients by name, many of their families having shopped there for generations.

'Good morning, Lord so-and-so, and how is her Ladyship?' was a not uncommon greeting. On the ground floor towards the back was a barber's shop where one could have a shave – wet of course – and a trim, including nasal hairs if you so wished. As loose hairs were being brushed off and you were helped on with your jacket you would be asked, 'And would sir like something for the weekend?'

Dod's attire was completed with a breast pocket handkerchief, white for work and coloured silk for other occasions, together with highly-polished black leather shoes. He wrote with a silver fountain pen and matching propelling pencil; and from a silver cigarette case would offer Senior Service cigarettes which he lit with a Ronson petrol cigarette lighter that usually worked at the fifth or sixth attempt. Dod's ensemble was accompanied by a tightly furled umbrella (which was never opened – even if it rained) and a bowler hat for wearing in the city.

Woog had been to a preparatory school in the south of the city where boys were beaten for being stupid and boxing was compulsory. Woog was a clever boy – once winning the 'longest word you can spell' competition with 'antidisestablishmentarianism'. He was not so good at boxing and regularly received the boxing equivalent of 'could do better' on his report.

It may have been because of the beatings and the boxing (or more probably because we had moved to the north of Norwich) that I was sent to St Christopher's preparatory school in Catton. This was a soft option by comparison. There were no beatings or boxing – and there were girls. I fell head over heels in love with two of them and started to learn to play the piano. After three years there I surprised both myself and my parents by passing the entrance examination for King Edward VI school, where I joined the Woog, who was four years ahead of me, and became 'Howard minor'. The school was situated in the cathedral close, and as the Norwich Union head office where Dod worked was adjacent, Dod drove us to school until we were old enough to cycle.

We were always late, or always *nearly* late. Dod would blame the car, the traffic or other drivers for being too slow but the real reason (I soon discovered) was simple: we left home too late. After a rushed breakfast, the first challenge Dod had was starting the car, a black Austin A30. It seems amazing now that this was often a difficult and time-consuming job, particularly in winter. The car was normally parked in a lane at the back of the garden, since the wooden gates to the garage had long ago ceased working and were jammed closed. Dod first had to judge the climatic conditions, which he did by looking toward the sky for a moment or two with both arms extended and hands held palm upwards. Dod then climbed into the car, settled into the driver's seat, pulled the choke out about half an inch and with a whispered, 'Come on, old girl,' turned the key in the ignition. Nothing would happen on the first couple of attempts and then the engine usually turned over a few times but would fail to start and Dod would turn the ignition off, saying, with his head half turned toward Woog and me in the back seat, 'Mustn't flatten the battery.' This procedure was then repeated with minute adjustments to the choke until either the engine started or the battery became flat. If the engine coughed a bit and some smoke appeared from the exhaust, Dod would comment, 'Ah, she nearly caught then,' usually followed quickly by 'Damn, I've flooded her,' as all signs of engine activity ceased. Amazingly, the car would eventually start and we then had about five minutes to complete the journey from the back of No.3 to the side door of the Cathedral where Assembly was held – a distance of about two miles – in just under five minutes. This was clearly impossible, even in an Austin A30, but Dod would try to make it by taking a series of shortcuts.

Traffic was generally light down Constitution Hill but would build up on Magdalen Road before the Artichoke traffic lights, where we needed to turn left. If there was a significant queue here, and the lights had just turned to red, Dod would make the decision to take his favourite shortcut. At the last possible moment, he would suddenly turn to the left, up either Beaconsfield or Marlborough Road, depending on how long the queue was. Both those roads were steep hills, with cars parked on either side, so that there was only room for a single car and the gamble was that nothing would be coming down the hill. At the top, a sharp right turn took us all the way down Spencer Street and brought us to Bull Close Road, the road we would have been on if we hadn't taken the short cut. Strictly speaking, this was not a short cut, more of a long cut, as it was about three times as long as the direct route. As we attempted to re-enter the traffic, Dod occasionally spotted a car which we had managed to get in front of by this manoeuvre and would cry triumphantly, 'There you go! We've gained on him.' We then drove along Whitefriars past the Jarrolds depository, over the River Wensum, and along by the Bishop's Palace to Palace Street, where we would join another queue. All of this would be would be negotiated as fast as possible with numerous exclamations of, 'It's like Piccadilly Circus on a Pancake Tuesday,' or 'Am I fast, or is everyone else slow?' until we were close enough to the school for us to jump out and run the rest of the way, through the Erpingham gate, into the close and then into the Cathedral. Woog and I were grateful when we became old enough to cycle to school and avoid this daily farce.

Nowadays I believe afternoon tea is only served at Reid's Hotel in Funchal and until recently on the Q.E.2. In the sixties this ritual was also observed at No.3 and was one of Dod's favourite institutions. At four o'clock on Saturdays and Sundays we would all sit down in the front room and Dod would carry the dishes in on a silver tray. A silver tea service was accompanied by cups and saucers along with dainty sandwiches and cakes. The latter would be placed on the cake stand. This was one of those elegant pieces of Edwardian mahogany furniture with three rimmed platforms held between two long legs, each with two feet, and with everything joined neatly at the top by a handle. The platforms were hinged so that they could fold down when not in use, the stand being placed flat against the wall. Like most of our furniture it was past its best and the locking hinge was broken. Occasionally we had guests for tea and it was when Uncle Wally (not his real name) and Auntie Polly (not her real name) came round for tea, that the stand spontaneously collapsed for the first time, depositing on the floor sandwiches and cream cakes, along with Zompie's home-made rock cakes. I must confess that initially Woog and I saw the humour of this, but a quick look at Dod's face wiped the smirks off our faces, as he blamed Zomp for not putting the stand up properly. Wally and Polly made light of this little setback. It was therefore particularly unfortunate that immediately the cakes had been replaced on the re-erected stand, Wally selected one of Zompie's home made rock cakes, bit into it with enthusiasm and broke a tooth. He was a kind, generous man and tried to disguise the event for a while, but the unmistakable clink as the tooth fell onto his plate and the un-missable gap where the tooth had previously been, made it obvious what had happened. Zompie was horrified that her cake could have had such a destructive effect, but Wally – always the gentleman – explained that he had weak teeth, and that the cake was delicious. When Woog mischievously offered him another one, however, he politely declined.

On one winter evening after tea, as we were sitting by a blazing fire, the front doorbell rang. Zomp said, 'I wonder who that could be?' and, as none of us could guess, Dod decided the only way to find out was to go and open the front door. It was a good job he did, as outside he found a complete stranger who informed us that our house was on fire. Sure enough, when we had all piled out and as we stood on the pavement, we could see several feet of flames shooting impressively from our chimney.

'That shouldn't happen,' said Dod, and, after thanking the passer-by, phoned for the fire-brigade. By now a small crowd had gathered outside No. 3 and Zompie had started to distribute rock cakes to the onlookers. The fire engine duly arrived with some large firemen, one of whom put his helmet on my head (which was excellent fun and made the whole episode worthwhile as far as I was concerned) while the others clambered up to the roof, poured some water down the chimney and rapidly extinguished the fire at the cost of a considerable mess in the sitting room. The head firemen asked Dod when the chimney had last been swept.

Dod said he couldn't be sure, which sounded better than 'never' – which was probably much nearer the truth.

Dod had rather a thing about fires. Every so often he would have a bonfire in the garden. Like starting the car, getting the fire going would take hours, involving lots of newspapers and matches. Once Dod had it well alight he would then promptly extinguish it by putting lots of wet green leaves and grass cuttings on top, the smouldering of which produced a dense fog that, if the wind was in the right direction, would reduce visibility in Wall Road to dangerous levels, and induce wheezing and coughing amongst those queuing for the number 89 bus, whose terminus was there. During one particularly fine bonfire, visibility was so poor that neither Dod nor I could see the fence at the end of our garden, a distance of only a few yards. As we watched the smoke spiral upwards I heard someone shouting. Dod and I peered through the smoke and eventually identified a man wearing a peaked cap, with a ticket machine hanging from his neck. He was standing on the other side of the fence, waving his arms and yelling. On closer inspection he turned out to be a bus conductor. With remarkable composure, and in between fits of coughing, he explained that the bus driver couldn't see far enough to drive down Wall Road and asked us if we wouldn't awfully mind putting the fire out.

Although nylon stockings had been introduced during the war it wasn't until the sixties that Zompie discovered other nylon goods. The worst inventions by far were the nylon sheets – later superseded by the only slightly less lethal brushed nylon sheet – and the nylon shirt. These items were acquired because they were easy to wash and dry, and above all did not need ironing, Zompie's least favourite job. Indeed, if you tried to iron them they melted. The down-side was the electromagnetic properties of these items – they built up static. After a night sleeping between a pair of nylon sheets, so much static built up that overnight your hair curled. In the morning whenever you got out of bed, the first part of your body that touched another object such as the floor discharged this energy with a loud crack, thus causing considerable discomfort to the affected anatomical region. Everything you touched for the first hour or two of the day created a spark and a shock.

The nylon shirt had a similar effect of making you spark every time you touched something, while at the same time the shirt developed a ghostly luminescence which in a darkened room could be quite disturbing to those of an impressionable disposition. They also made you very sweaty. We implored Zomp to go back to cotton sheets and shirts – which she eventually did – a decision expedited by Dod burning numerous holes in his nylon sheets while smoking in bed, nearly setting the house on fire for a second time.

CHAPTER 4: HOME AFFAIRS

Dod's wedding to Shirley Warren Parkinson drew a small crowd to St. Nicholas's church Wallasey on July 22nd, 1945. This still being wartime, the bells were not rung. I have to confess that I have never understood why church bells could not be rung during the war. I can hardly imagine that the Luftwaffe were waiting expectantly for the sound of wedding bells so that they could jump into their planes and then bomb the happy couple. Perhaps it was part of the German master-plan, a sort of wedding-day genocide. Anyway, three years after the event, Woog was born, followed five years later by me.

Dod didn't believe that women should work, or have an opinion, and would have agreed with the American wit who stated that 'A woman's place is in the oven,' and similar views were held about Woog and myself. 'Little boys should be seen but not heard,' he told us many times when we were noisy. Zompie was a bright, intelligent, but down-trodden woman who as a result lacked social confidence. Having a bigoted husband and two noisy boys didn't help. At school and as a signaller in the A.T.S. she had been a pretty, lively girl but was never overtly fashion-conscious.

Dod's lifestyle wasn't conducive to a social life for Zomp as it was centred around pubs and his male friends. I cannot ever recall a dinner party at No. 3 and we rarely entertained there. It was however quite a large house to run and maintain. The day-to-day work of cleaning, shopping, and cooking kept Zomp busy but there was also the small ornamental front garden and a long back garden to be maintained. At the back of the house, french doors – above which was a candy-striped canvas retractable awning – opened from the dining room on to an ornamental area set with a lawn and flowerbeds. Half-way down the path, which ran the length of the garden, was a sundial and a rickety, rustic wooden bench. Beyond was an orchard planted with apple, pear, cherry and Victoria plum trees, between which ran little paths marked out with terracotta tiles. There were also gooseberry and raspberry bushes with a crab-apple tree at the very end, in front of the garage and the air raid shelter. All in all, this was a classic Edwardian confection which had previously been well-maintained. Dod was never a keen gardener and the gardens and garage at the back soon fell into a state of disrepair. This was great for Woog and me for whom this formed a jungle in which to have adventures. From the back door of the house to the end of the back garden was a distance of about seventy-five yards. Woog and I would race up the uneven path along the side of the garden past the bamboo plant, through the orchard to the air-raid shelter and on to the back fence. For some bizarre reason Woog called this 'investing'. While playing near the back of the house, without warning Woog would suddenly shout, 'Let's invest!' upon which we both hared down the path. It wasn't really a case of winning: it was the process that was important. Out of breath at the end of the garden, Woog would usually say, 'That was a good invest' and just as I was agreeing he would suddenly add, 'Let's invest back' and set off back down the path with me trailing behind.

* * *

The man Thompson was our neighbour's odd-job man and he had always been old. At about five foot six, he was short and looked even shorter, being stooped and unable to straighten his back. He had a large head, permanently tilted to the right, on which he wore a flat cap which had originally been a greenish-tweedy colour. His nose was enormous, with coarse black hairs growing from the tip. He always wore an open-necked shirt under a black waistcoat below which were a pair of baggy trousers held up by braces. Bright brown eyes twinkled and looked out from his deeply-lined and weather-beaten face. He had worked for our neighbours at No. 5, the Chittocks, for many years and when we first moved in to No. 3 he must have already been sixty-five years old. He was the odd-job man *par excellence.* A Norwich man born and bred, he had been a cobbler to trade and as a young man had fought in Mesopotamia during the First World War. For many years he had looked after the Chittocks next door. Old Mr Chittock had been a widower for numerous years and young Mr C – a confirmed batchelor – showed no sign of ever marrying, although he had been seen with a lady friend on one or two occasions. Dod reckoned Mr. C. was 'worth a bob or two'.

We hadn't lived in No. 3 for very long when old Mr Chittock died at a good age. One Saturday when Dod was in the garden, young Mr Chittock shouted over the fence, 'Father died on Wednesday.'

'Oh! I'm so sorry,' Dod responded and there followed a polite discussion about him being a good age, and how it was really a kindness, ending with the philosophical remark, 'It'll come to us all sooner or later' from Dod. As Dod turned to leave, young Mr C. said, 'Would you like to pay your respects?'

'I would be pleased to. When is it?' asked Dod, referring to the forthcoming funeral.

'Any time you like, but just give me half an hour's notice so I can take the lid off,' came the unexpected reply. After a while it dawned on Dod that old Mr C. was lying in state. This proved to be the case, and the chosen venue was the dining room, a room kept for special occasions such as this. After saying he would be round later in the day, Dod went indoors and found Zompie.

'You'll never guess what, dear,' he said excitedly, 'Old Mr Chittock has died and is lying in state on the dining room table next door! We've been invited round to pay our respects.'

Zomp was quite taken aback. She had suspected the inevitable had occurred as the old boy had not been seen for a while, and the curtains of No. 5 had remained drawn since Wednesday, but she was uneasy about the fact of a dead body lying next door, whatever state it was in.

'Oh no, I couldn't, I just couldn't. You'll have to go on your own; tell him that I have to look after the boys.'

Dod agreed that this was not the ideal occasion for a family outing, and resigned himself to the fact that he would have to go round on his own and pay respects on behalf of us all. At the appointed time that evening, dressed smartly in a three piece charcoal-coloured suit, Dod, with considerable trepidation, went to the front door of No. 5 and rang the bell. This was a new social experience for Dod and he unsure of the etiquette. He had discussed with Zomp whether or not it was necessary to bring a token gift. Zomp wondered if Dod should take some flowers; Woog helpfully suggested chocolates and Dod thought something alcoholic might be apposite; but after considerable discussion we all agreed that no gifts were necessary. Old Mr.Thompson opened the door. He looked strange and Dod realised this was because of the absence of his cap, respectfully removed for the occasion. Behind him stood young Mr C. who was in hearty good form. There had already been several visitors to view the body throughout the day and each time he had partaken of a small sherry or two with his guests, so that by now he was quite jolly.

'Come on in, Bill, come on in. It's good of you to come round,' he said as he uncharacteristically put his arm round Dod's shoulder and added, 'Dad's body's in here,' followed by a small belch which smelled strongly of sweet sherry.

Dod entered the darkened room where, in the middle, the mortal remains of old Mr Chittock were laid out in an open coffin on the dining room table. Young Mr. C. and Thompson dutifully held back, Dod advanced toward the coffin and when about a yard away clasped his hands together as though in prayer and bowed his head towards the corpse. After what seemed like ages to him but in reality was probably only ten seconds, he moved back, bowed his head again, turned around, and made to leave the room. He was accordingly ushered through the hall into the kitchen and handed a small sherry while he struggled for something appropriate to say. 'He looks very peaceful,' Dod said at last, adding 'Russell' after a lengthy pause. He had never been on Christian name terms with young Mr Chittock but this now seemed an appropriate time to address him by his first name.

'Yes he's at peace now – at peace'. Russell by now had finished his sherry and Thompson, who was much more comfortable having donned his cap again, was topping up his glass. The doorbell rang and Thompson took off his cap and as he and young Mr C. headed once more towards the front door, with muttered condolences, Dod took the opportunity to empty his glass and make his exit.

After old man Chittock's death, Thompson started doing some odd jobs for us. The garage door had been jammed shut for many years. During a cross-fence chat Dod had mentioned this to young Mr Chittock – who retained this title even though there was no extant old Mr Chittock any more – and a few days later Thompson knocked at the back door. Dod opened it and on seeing Thompson said, 'Hello, Mr Thompson. It's nice to see you. What brings you round?' Here was a man you would never call by his first name in – fact Woog and I suspected that he didn't have one. He would forever be simply 'Thompson', 'The man Thompson' or, when we were older, 'Tommy'.

'Mr Chittock said you have a problem with your garage door,' he said in his broad Norwich accent. 'I was wonderin' if you wanted me to fix that for you?'

Dod had been unable to open the door for years and responded enthusiastically, 'I would be delighted if you could fix it. Just let me know what you need and how much it will cost.'

'That's all right then, I'll measure up next week sometime,' and with that he left.

For Dod the task was as good as done. All that had to happen was for Thompson to measure up and then do the job. Two weeks at the outside, thought Dod, and the car would be in the garage for the first time in years.

Some weeks later, when there hadn't been any obvious progress, Dod saw Thompson in the Chittock's garden, 'How's it going?' He asked. 'When do you think you'll be able to fix the garage?'

'I need to measure up first, I'll do that next week when I've finished off the chicken-run here,' he replied.

Dod was disappointed that even stage one, the measuring up, had not been done – but clearly the chickens took priority. A few weeks later there came a knock at the back door and Zompie opened it. There stood Thompson. 'I've come to measure up,' he announced firmly.

'Oh, Bill will be *so* pleased. Would you like a cup of tea and a rock cake before you start?'

After tea and buns, Tommy then went off to measure up. Indeed he came round numerous times to measure up. Much tea was drunk and many rock cakes consumed, but progress was frustratingly slow. 'How much measuring up does he have to do?' Dod said in exasperation. Six months later he was still measuring up but suddenly, when we all thought it would never happen, the job was done, the garage door opened smoothly and the car could at last be driven inside.

CHAPTER 5: THE LESSON

King Edward VI School is situated within the magnificent surroundings of Norwich Cathedral Close. The main campus is sandwiched between the medieval buildings of the school chapel and the cathedral itself, although some classes used to be held in No. 68, a converted house in the close owned by the school. From the age of ten until I left school at seventeen, I was a chorister in the choir. This meant that during term time I sang at least one service each Sunday in the school chapel, a lovely medieval building with a wooden gallery at the back where the organ and the choir-stalls stood. The gallery was accessed by a narrow, creaky, wooden spiral staircase with a rope handrail to aid ascent. The noise of twenty or so choristers climbing these stairs was not inconsiderable and heralded the beginning of each service. Every Sunday we sang Matins, and there was Evensong once a month. Matins was held at ten in the morning, early enough for the boarders, who were strongly encouraged to attend, to have the rest of the day off for sport, visits, work or whatever else boarders got up to at weekends.

On Sundays Dod always gave me a lift to school, where I would join the rest of the choirboys in the library which was served as dressing-room for the occasion. Here we each donned a red cassock, ruff and surplice, recited a brief prayer and then processed noisily to the chapel and up the spiral stair to the choir gallery. Dod stayed for the service and drove me home afterwards: he had been a chorister himself and enjoyed the music. He was slightly deaf and would chose an unobtrusive pew near the back of the Chapel seated next to the wall so that he could be close to a radiator and quietly doze off during the sermon which all too often could be long and somewhat tedious.

Dod's regular attendance, albeit not entirely for the right reasons, was probably why he was asked to read one of the lessons. My recollection is that this happened some time toward the end of the spring term but I cannot be certain. What I am sure about is that it was not in the weeks leading up to Christmas. That was why, at the allotted time, after a dignified walk up the aisle to the lectern, it came as a distinct surprise to all of us in both the choir and the congregation to hear him start to read the Christmas story from St Luke. Like the true performer he was, once Dod had begun there was no turning back, and he continued as though nothing was wrong. In deep and sonorous tones he retailed the story of the severe shortage of rooms in Bethlehem, the subsequent virgin birth and the consequent babe in a manger – all of this in the weeks leading up to Easter. In retrospect it is clear that there would have been no prior indication as to when he should end the reading, so I presume Dod just stopped when he felt he had spoken for long enough, or at what he felt was a suitable juncture. Anyway, just as the wise men were approaching Bethlehem, he decided that the reading should end and, with great aplomb, he gently and carefully closed the massive and ancient bible, thereby making it impossible for the reader of the second lesson to find his place. Dod then raised his eyes from the lectern, gazed heavenwards and, with an expansive gesture, took off his half-moon glasses, proudly uttered, 'Thanks be to God,' and walked slowly back to his pew.

By this stage, both the Headmaster and the Canon taking the service were looking somewhat stunned. Neither had had any idea how much of St Luke's Christmas story they were going to get, and for all they knew Dod might have attempted the whole Gospel; and so, when he had finished, they had to do their best to continue and attempt to make some sense of the service. Back in his pew, Dod waited expectantly for the next hymn as though nothing in the least untoward had happened.

In the years that followed, Dod would admit that his reading had not been entirely apposite for the time of year and he would imply that there had been some act of sabotage, with the book mark deliberately placed at the wrong page of the Bible. Why anyone should have wanted to do such a thing I have no idea!

After the service Dod would wait for me outside the chapel, strolling around the cathedral close smoking cigarettes while nodding benignly to other Chapel-goers and parents. He also had to try to avoid the Bursar. Dod was usually a term or two behind with the school fees and the Bursar was also a regular Chapel-goer. He would sidle up to Dod and, after a preliminary chat about the service, mention in passing that Dod was behind with the fees and that payment would be appreciated. Upon hearing this Dod would feign surprise and say, 'My dear Bursar, I had no idea! Good job I bumped into you.' Dod then did absolutely nothing about it until the scene was solemnly re-enacted some other Sunday, when he would continue to do nothing about it.

Most Sundays there would be a discussion at home about how the service had gone.

'Was it a nice service, dear?' Zomp would ask,

'Very good. The choir sang very well – what was that introit, old boy?'

'Breathe on me Breath of God – Tertius Noble' I smartly replied on that occasion.

'Ah, yes. I thought I recognised it. Used to sing that many years ago. That tenor had a lovely voice.'

'That's Richard Swift,' Zomp remarked having known his mother; 'he's got a choral scholarship to Cambridge.'

'Lovely voice. You know, dear, the Burser caught me again today. I really must do something about the school fees.'

The school choir used to sing at services in many of the beautiful medieval churches which are dotted about Norfolk, to small congregations often of only three or four people. On one occasion I recall there was no congregation at all but the service went ahead regardless of that. On those outings, a coach took us back to school, still in our deep red cassocks and white surplices topped with a frilly ruff, there to change back into our school uniforms, to await collection by our parents.

Returning from one of these trips, I made a major error of judgement. We were on the Wroxham road on the outskirts of the city and the coach was pulling up at a red traffic light when I saw Dod walking alongside on the pavement. I didn't think to ask myself why Dod was there when he should have been at school waiting for me but without hesitation I asked the driver to let me off. Still in full chorister regalia, I then walked up to the complete stranger whom I had mistaken for Dod. True, he was grey-haired and tall, but that was where the resemblance ended. I am not sure which of us was the more startled. The man was certainly surprised by the sudden appearance of a choirboy calling him Dad in the middle of a busy street on a Saturday afternoon. The seriousness of the situation now being apparent to me, I was now in a bit of a pickle. My uniform was at school where Dod would be waiting and I was about three miles away dressed as a choirboy. There was no choice but to run for it. For some reason it never occurred to me to take off my chorister's robes, and unthinkingly, I just started to run. Though I was quite a fast runner, I quickly learned why the cassock was not the chosen garment for athletics. I ran along the Wroxham Road for about a mile, turned right on reaching the ring road, and after another mile turned left into Constitution Hill and so to home, attracting quite a lot of attention en route. Zomp was in, and not a little surprised when I arrived, while Dod arrived back shortly after, having been made aware of the situation when the bus returned to school without me.

It is perhaps because of escapades such as this that Zomp did not have the utmost confidence in me. I certainly did not perform well at school.

Dod said, 'Don't worry, dear. Winnie (as he always referred to his hero Winston Churchill) was hopeless at school, and only developed later in life'. It was true that in general the Howards were late developers – some so late they never noticeably developed at all. The implication seemed to be that if Winston Churchill had not been good at school and had been a late developer, then I was sure be a good wartime leader in later years if one should be needed. Zompie was not entirely convinced by this argument. I duly sat the eleven-plus exam, presumably when I was eleven. Some weeks later the results came by post and Zomp immediately went upstairs to open the letter and confirm the bad news in the privacy of her bedroom; I timidly followed her in. She was standing by the window with the letter in her hand, looking distinctly peplexed.

'What does it say, Mum?' I asked.

'It says here that you've passed!' she answered in a quiet and slightly puzzled tone.

It was only some years later that I found out that Zomp had subsequently telephoned the Education Department to confirm the result, as she thought there must certainly have been some mistake. Accordingly I graduated from the junior to the senior school and gradually moved up the ranks, heading toward the inevitability of O-level examinations. Life at No. 3 continued, term after term, interrupted only by holidays and festivities.

CHAPTER 6: DOD ON VACATION

As young children we didn't go abroad for our holidays. In the fifties and sixties few people left the safety of Britain's shores and only the wealthy could afford to do so. My friend Robin went to Spain with his family – but they had lots of money. They had a large house in Hellesdon, just outside Norwich, and his father owned a Jaguar. I later learned that when they went away they took a caravan, so that didn't really count as a proper holiday abroad.

Easter and summer holidays were spent in Wallasey, where both sets of grandparents lived. Strictly speaking, we didn't have a full set of grandparents, as both grandfathers had died a good while before I was born, but our two Grannies still lived in Wallasey in their family homes. Granny Parky, who was Zompie's mother, lived in Oldfield Road and had the larger house, so this was where we children stayed, while Dod used to walk a mile or so down the road to Groveland Road where Granny Howard lived, to spend the night there. Both houses were fun. Granny Parky's had an outside toilet in which you could lock yourself and the older boys could have a smoke, but for me Granny Howard's was better, as she had fairies at the bottom of her garden. It was where the coastal train line ran; and she made chips.

On the occasion of those holidays we used to drive from Norwich to Wallasey in Dod's black Austin A30. This journey of about three hundred miles was a major undertaking. A week or so before the holiday, Dod would get the car serviced. The night before, it (or 'she' as Dod preferred to call her) would be filled with petrol, the oil and tyres checked, and Zomp prepared a picnic. Finally Woog would work out the itinerary. I have never understood why he did this, but being five years younger than my brother I thought he was very clever. Very sensibly, he would work backwards from the desired time of arrival. When

Woog asked her what time she wanted to arrive Zomp would say, 'Oh, about five would be nice, in time for tea.' This was of course hopelessly optimistic as we had never been known to arrive anything earlier than late at night.

'Bill, it would be nice to arrive a bit earlier this year, wouldn't it? Why don't we try to get a nice early start?'

Dod would agree, and Woog would dutifully draw up his itinerary. This would have a start time, and the estimated time of arrival at key points, usually Swaffham, Kings Lynn, Peterborough, Leicester, and so on; together with an estimate of when and where we would stop for lunch and other essential comfort breaks. Woog calculated that to arrive at five p.m. the time of departure would need to be six in the morning, necessitating our getting up at five a.m. The plan was therefore already fundamentally flawed, as none of us had got up that early since Dod had been discharged from the army. At eight in the morning we would still be packing the car and trying to force more into the small boot than it was designed to take.

The Austin A30 had a very small boot, curving both downwards and inwards, and packing it was a bit like argifying – only Dod could do it. Dod first attempted to get all the suitcases in and when they wouldn't fit they would all be removed and put on the road. He then replaced them in the boot in a different order; and when, not surprisingly, they still wouldn't fit in, he repeated the exercise several times over until all possible combinations had been tried. Only then would he admit that the boot wasn't big enough. The bags were then removed again, put on the road and some repacking done. Eventually, and after combining the contents of some of the cases and discarding non-essential items, the boot lid would be closed. This process took a good half-hour or more, time not allowed for in the Woog's itinerary. Finally, we would finish breakfast and set off just before nine o'clock if we were lucky. Thus, even before the engine was started, Woog's schedule was totally wrecked. As we reached the top of Constitution Hill, Woog would usually comment that we should be close to Kings Lynn by now, resigned to the fact that his timetable would never work.

'Never mind, we can make the time up later,' was Dod's stock answer. This also never happened. I am unsure what speed Woog used in his calculations but it was clearly more than an Austin A30 was capable of, by a good margin. On reaching Swaffham, the first checkpoint on our journey, Dod would normally discuss progress with Woog. 'How are we doing, old boy?'

'We should have been here two hours ago,' would come the reply and in a bizarrely optimistic interpretation of this fact, Dod's response inevitably was, 'Oh well, that's fine. We're keeping up and we can always make up time later on' – which we never did – or he would say, 'I'll two hours you!' Woog and I never completely understood why, when lost for words, Dod would respond in such a fashion but it was generally perceived to be slightly threatening and an end to any dialogue.

Dod and Zomp then chatted cheerfully and smoked cigarettes in the front of the car while Woog and I fought together. The dispute was generally about back-seat territory. While we were trying to get comfortable (by no means easy in the back of an A30) one of us would inadvertently stray across the midline of the rear seat, prompting a loud cry of, 'He's in my half again, Mum,' from the aggrieved party, followed by, 'He started it by coming into my half.' Cross words would follow from Dod.

'If you don't stop fighting, you can walk the rest of the way.' Woog said that Dod didn't really mean it but I was worried because it was a long way home and I was quite sure I'd get lost.

I don't think Dod owned a road map. He navigated by means of his sense of smell and an intimate knowledge of most of the public houses on the route. In the back, our games and daydreaming were frequently interrupted by observations such as, 'Ah, there's the Red Lion, dear, so we're on the right road and I think we're here earlier than last year. Next stop is the Railway Tavern, where we turn off to that other road… the A whatever it is.' Zomp said she thought it was the A47, and sometimes suggested that it might be helpful to have a map. Dod always disagreed. 'I know the road perfectly well and don't need any jolly old map to tell me how to get to Wallasey.'

It was hardly surprising therefore that we often got lost. Dod never admitted to being *really* lost, just to being what he called 'off track'. On such occasions he would drive around until he recognised something – usually a pub.

'Ah, there's The Dog and Duck. I know where we are now, dear; we're on the right track.' Sometimes, just to make sure, Dod would go into the pub to confirm his whereabouts This could take some time and he would come out smelling of beer.

'Rude to go in and not have a drink,' he'd explain.

Dod had a several strange ideas about pubs and drinking. His father had taught him that you should *never* leave a pub on an uneven number of pints. Grandfather had never explained why but clearly Dod was not willing to take the risk to find out. This policy did have certain drawbacks. If you were in a group and someone got ahead or behind in terms of numbers of pints, or arrived late, this could mean that you might never be able to leave since someone or other would always be on an uneven number – either that or else you left at separate times. It was also seen to be unlucky to leave a pub while it was raining. Sometimes I wonder how Dod ever managed to get out of a pub at all.

By one o'clock or so we were always hours behind schedule, Woog would throw his itinerary on the floor and stamp on it, while Dod said that we should start looking for somewhere to have lunch. We then would embark on a major detour to find what Zomp called 'a pleasant spot', with a field and preferably some tree cover for toilet purposes. This was easy for us males but more difficult for Zomp. Invariably, just as she was getting down to business – a car, or worse still a walker – would come into view and she had to pretend to be picking daisies.

Lunch was generally hard-boiled eggs (which Woog always said were bad) pork pies which were full of fresh air, and spam sandwiches, or corned beef if we were really lucky. On trips to the coast all those provisions would be mixed with liberal quantities of sand or grit. Dod and Zomp drank sweet coffee from a leaky thermos flask which they had used for the last fifteen years.

With the comment, 'Ah, that's better! I think we should press on now,' from Dod, Woog and I would climb into the back of the car and start fighting afresh as we attempted to find our way back to the main road. In the search for somewhere nice for our picnic we would frequently stray miles off the beaten track and hence would now be three or four hours behind schedule.

Eventually we would pass through Leicester, with its slabbed clipperty-clopperty roads, and on to the Potteries. 'Wouldn't like to live here!' Zomp said every year without fail; and so on to Cheshire where Woog, on seeing the white and black metal fencing, would announce that this was Cheshire fencing, and inform us that the fencing had been put up to keep the Cheshire Cat in the county. And so on to Wallasey where eventually we would arrive at Oldfield Road in the late evening darkness and Granny Parky with our Scottish cousins, Warren and Janice, would greet us before we could gratefully go to bed.

Holidays – and trips to the seaside – were somehow inextricably connected with ozone. Whenever there might be ozone about, Dod would breathe in deeply through his nose and say, 'Ah, just smell the ozone!' and then exhale slowly through his mouth. Apparently ozone was good for you. I was never sure why, but it was – because Dod said so.

When on holiday we always tried to find some ozone to

34

smell. The promenade at New Brighton was a good place for ozone-smelling and we always went there on the final day of our holiday, On one such occasion Dod drove us to the promenade for a last final health-giving smell. The weather was foul, with gale force onshore winds, and the tide was in. Dod got out of the car and tried to entice the rest of us on to the promenade. Zomp decided there was quite enough ozone to be had in the car, and Woog and I agreed. Not to be put off, Dod walked right up to the sea wall and assumed his ozone-smelling position, which involved standing up straight, with his back slightly arched and with hands on hips. He then breathed in deeply through his nose and started to exhale through his mouth. It was unfortunate that just at this moment a massive wave crashed against the sea wall, sending a huge column of water high into the air to come crashing down on to the promenade just where Dod was standing. How we laughed! Dod – now with sea water dripping off him – looked slightly annoyed at first but soon regained his normal composure and climbed back into the car remarking, 'Ah, I feel better for that! Nothing wrong with a bit of spray. You should have got out of the car, dear. It would have done you a power of good,' looking accusingly at Zomp as though she'd let him down.

Dod never let adverse weather conditions spoil his enjoyment. Whenever we went to the Norfolk coast he would don his swimming trunks and sit on the beach, regardless of cold, wind or rain. I vividly remember him seated by the sea wall at Caister in the pouring rain in his swimming trunks, sipping a pint of beer under an umbrella, while the rest of us sheltered in a nearby café.

A regular feature of our Wallasey holidays was 'Grannie's Ben'. This was short for Grannie's Benefit and involved setting up a stall on the pavement outside Granny Parky's house. To obtain items for the stall, Woog and our cousin Warren would seek out trinkets from the house. Usually these were obtained with the owner's consent, but if this couldn't be done it was no problem, since the owner of the purloined item could always buy it back for sixpence. Everything was sixpence and the proceeds went to Granny. The fact that all the items for sale came from her in the first place didn't seem to matter. Woog always reckoned that Warren was the favourite grandchild as he was the first, and had acne. I have no idea if this was true or not, but he certainly did have spots, had to use special soap, and was not allowed to eat chocolate – which seemed very harsh to me.

Another of Woog's wizard money-making schemes was to make cigarettes for Granny. He bought a Rizla cigarette-rolling machine, some filters and a small amount of tobacco, and would proceed to make a tidy profit selling these to Granny. Occasionally he would put a matchstick head half way down the cigarette. When Granny unsuspectingly lit up one of the trick fags we would gather close by. How we laughed when her cigarette exploded half way through and her hair caught fire! Granny Parky had a pronounced yellow streak on the front of her hair from smoking and was obviously a good customer. The only problem was that while she smoked Howard's Exploding Specials she couldn't continue to collect her Kensitas cigarette tokens. As the gifts she was smoking for were toys for us, there was something of a conflict of interest. The dilemma was resolved by always offering her one of her own Kensitas cigarettes as soon as she had finished a Howard Special. I don't know what Granny died of but I am sure her health was not improved by our visits. Collecting vouchers was all the rage and at that time Zompie collected Green Shield Stamps. These were then stuck into a slim book and when you had accumulated what seemed about a million books you loaded them onto the back of a dumper truck and took them to the Green Shield Stamp shop where they could be exchanged for a gift. The choice was not wide, but after collecting for a year or two you could probably aspire to a stainless steel toast rack

– or perhaps a pencil sharpener. The best way to build up the number of stamps you needed for one of those life-enhancing gifts was to buy petrol from an appropriately affiliated garage. Unfortunately, not all garages offered the inducement of these stamps and, when we were running low on fuel, Zompie would insist that we pass garage after garage to the point of running out of petrol until we found one that offered Green Shield Stamps.

The journey back from Wallasey to Norwich was a mirror-image of the journey out, except that after the Easter holidays, Woog and I would have the Easter egg packaging to play with. With the chocolate long gone, the packages were huge fun and could be space ships, cars, submarines or clubs to hit each other with. This would often keep us amused for the first ten miles of the three hundred mile journey. Woog never bothered to make an itinerary for the return journey.

When Zomp asked Woog, 'Why don't you do one of your schedules, dear?' he quite understandably replied that there was no point in it when we were chronically unable even to start the journey anywhere near the correct time. In fact, if anything the return journey was worse, since the amount of luggage increased (as it always does on a holiday) and we had our goodbyes to say – which could take a good half-hour. One thing was essential: we had to get to Swaffham before ten o'clock for fish and chips. This was necessary as the only cooker we had at home was the Aga, which could take upwards of twelve hours before it reached cooking temperature – and that was only if Dod's relighting ritual worked first time round.

We did go abroad once, when we were older, to Spain: to Malgrat de Mar, which is on one of the Costas. It was the first time any of us had been in an aeroplane. We left from Luton Airport and Woog and I were hugely excited as we strapped ourselves into the seats. Woog said we would have to reach over a hundred miles an hour to take off. We had never exceeded sixty miles an hour in the Morris Minor which Dod then had. As the plane accelerated down the runway and we were forced back into our seats, Woog said, 'Feel that phenomenal g force!' I had no idea what he was talking about but agreed.

'Wow! Phenomenal!!'

This was the first time abroad for us and Woog spent the first day getting badly sunburned and had to spend the next few days in the hotel room we shared, where he became badly constipated and consequently blocked the toilet.

Dod said that just because we were on holiday and in a foreign land we shouldn't let standards slip, so he insisted that we dress for dinner wearing a tie and jacket. Zompie wore her specially bought, flowery, flouncy summer dress which was cut just low enough to show a glimpse of cleavage on which rested her string of pearls. Dod himself dressed in the style of a character from a Graham Greene novel or Somerset Maugham short story. He wore a newly purchased cream-coloured linen jacket, white tropical trousers (he refused to call them slacks) and his old school tie. If he'd had one, I'm sure he would have also worn a Panama hat. He could well have been Our Man in Havana but the problem was that this was a package holiday and he was our man in a downmarket hotel in Malgrat de Mar. Not only were we the only diners wearing jackets, but many guests weren't even wearing shirts. Dod led us across the dining room to our table, nodding and smiling to the other guests and muttering 'Good evening' as he passed by their tables. Woog and I followed self-consciously, our eyes fixed firmly on the ground. When we reached our table, Dod pulled out a seat for Zomp and we all sat down. Woog and I felt relieved that the attention on us would now subside. Dod looked around, nodded to our neighbours at the next table and, with an expansive smile, said, 'Well, this is jolly nice.' As we settled down to our dinner Zomp, with great poise and understatement, said, 'I think it might not be necessary for the boys to wear a jacket for dinner in future, Bill.'

Indeed, after this first experience Dod did relax the dress code for Woog and myself but still insisted on wearing a collar, tie and jacket at dinner for the rest of the holiday.

Apart from this – and a couple of trips to Jersey when we were older – our holidays were invariably spent in Norwich; and Christmas in particular was a highly anticipated event at No. 3.

CHAPTER 7: FESTIVE DOD

We all celebrated Christmas well in the Howard household and none more so than Dod. Christmas is a time of rituals and we certainly had many at No. 3 Constitution Hill. The first of these was the setting up of the Christmas tree. To start with, Dod always bought a tree which was far too big for the space for which it was intended – which was the hallway near the front door. After some careful pruning, Dod put the tree in a special pot he kept for the job, stabilised the whole structure by tying it to the stair banisters with a few pieces of string, and then the tree would be in position ready for dressing about a week before Christmas Day. Then followed the ritual of trying to get the tree lights to work. These were ancient. A decided fire-risk, they never worked first time. Dod draped them around the tree in an artistic fashion and then with great ceremony he would flick the switch, upon which the lights should have lit up. Nothing ever happened at this first attempt. 'That's strange, they were definitely working when I put them away last Christmas', Dod pronounced every year, seemingly genuinely surprised at this turn of events.

The tree-lights ritual would then begin in real earnest. Each bulb would be unscrewed, peered at intensely, shaken a bit and then screwed back into its holder. These bulbs were large by modern standards, and were wired in serial, which meant that if there was a fault in one they all stayed out. It also meant that you had no idea whatsoever which bulb was the faulty one. After half an hour or so of checking each bulb in this way they would flicker on, and then promptly go out again. This process would go on for an hour or so until the lights would stay on for a longer than a flicker, but still a decidedly finite period.

At frequent intervals during this ritual performance, Dod would declare, 'I suppose they *are* getting on a bit', and, 'Maybe we should get some new ones,' which he never did. Finally, when they all lit up and it appeared likely that they would remain lit, he would triumphantly remark, 'There! I told you they would work', upon which they would promptly go out again.

The lights then flickered on and off (not deliberately, like modern ones) for two weeks or so until the tree was taken down and they were put away, in working order; only for the whole scene to be re-enacted the following year. Once the lights were on the tree they were accompanied by baubles, tinsel and an ancient fairy, which was placed on the top of the tree. The story went that this doll had been given to Dod when he was a child – Lord knows why – and had been the main feature of the tree ever since. That would make the aged fairy about fifty at the time of which I am writing, and she looked every bit of it.

Little else happened until Christmas Eve. Everything was left until then. It was the day of Dod's office party and Zompie and I used to meet Dod in the Princes tea rooms for afternoon tea. From an early age I noticed that Dod's behaviour was often strange on these occasions; he seemed to have a certain difficulty with his balance and speech. I finally made a decision to stop meeting him on Christmas Eve after one occasion when he arranged to give Zompie and me a lift home. This was before the days of the breathalyser, at a time when one's capability to drive was simply assessed by the ability to walk along a chalk line drawn on the floor of the police station. By any standards Dod was not fit to drive. We met at about four in the afternnon in a car park on Market Hill, where he had left the car some hours earlier. I settled into the back seat of the Austin A30 and Zompie stationed herself in the front passenger seat as Dod climbed unsteadily into the driving seat. Before closing the door he leant over and threw up. He then muttered something about feeling much better, adding that he thought some of the food at the party might have been a bit off.

Zompie obviously didn't entirely agree with this assessment

of why Dod had been sick and asked him if he was feeling well enough to drive. This was like a red rag to a bull. To imply that Dod was not fit to drive was akin to insinuating that he was a communist, a homosexual or worst of all, a foreigner. 'Of course I am, dear,' was his emphatic response, as he proceeded to throw up for a second time.

There followed the most nightmarish car drive I have ever experienced. It was immediately clear that Dod's own assessment of his ability to drive had been incorrect. He had trouble keeping his head up, and when he did look up it was clear that both vision and coordination were completely shot. Conjugate gaze – the ability of both eyes to look in the same direction at any one time – had long been lost and physiologically Dod was functioning at a spinal level, which was hardly ideal for driving.

At that time Zompie could not drive. However, with much shouting she grabbed the steering wheel and guided the car along the highway, narrowly avoiding pedestrians, other cars, and stationary objects such as houses, Norwich Cathedral and the River Wensum. Other road users sounded their horns and gesticulated; and then, realising that these actions were ineffectual, pulled over, leapt out of their cars and ran for cover, while others, if they had time, turned off and took another route home. Pedestrians flattened themselves against walls or leapt into the relative safety of shop doorways. It was a bit like being in an emergency vehicle with a flashing blue light, only in this case the driver was the one who was ill and lay slumped with his head bowed for most of the journey. It was thus particularly bizarre that, on reaching the roundabout at the Mousehold end of Riverside Road, Dod raised his head, looked blearily through the windscreen and decided that we should take the longer, more picturesque route home across Mousehold Heath. Amazingly Zomp kept the car on the road and we zigzagged our way back to Constitution Hill.

In the days before Christmas there were numerous other rituals to be observed. The Christmas drinks had to be picked up from Backs, a licensed victualler on Judge's Walk. Dod always parked the car outside where it got in everyone's way and came out a little while later with a box full of bottles which usually included Crabbie's Green Ginger for Woog and myself. Generally a bottle or two would be dropped and broken during this transfer. Then there was the turkey (or 'the bird' as Dod preferred to call it) which had to be collected. For some strange reason this was ordered through a pub called The Prince of Wales, but better known as The Feathers, which was on King Street and conveniently close to Dod's office. In fact, he spent so much time there one could be forgiven for thinking it was his office. This was where Dod did his business entertaining, and as there were always clients and colleagues in the lounge bar he would inevitably have a few beers before bringing the bird back home.

In order to ensure that we would not run out of food over the festive period and to be able to eat turkey in one guise or another for a minimum of three weeks, Dod always bought a turkey weighing around twenty pounds. This caused a number of problems on the catering front. Firstly, the bird would often be too big to go into the oven and would require some adjustment to its shape before it would fit. A heavy blunt object, such as a small shovel or the First World War trenching tool we had somehow acquired, were ideal for this job. As I have previously mentioned, the only cooker we had was the Aga and the cooking time would vary between eighteen and twenty-four hours. It was not an exact science since the oven temperature depended on the wind direction and the ambient temperature of the backyard. Basically, the bird was squeezed into the oven on Christmas Eve and stayed there until the following afternoon, when we would stand around drinking Woog beer and gin and tonics until it was ready.

Woog beer was a lethal concoction which Woog brewed each Christmas. One year I bought him a plastic barrel from Boots to brew it in so as to avoid the labour of bottling. Prior to this innovation his bottles of beer all had an inch or more of sediment at the bottom which Dod reckoned was the sign of a good beer – but I was not so sure. If your hands were not entirely steady, it was possible to get more mouthfuls of sediment than of beer. The barrel overcame this problem as there was a gutter to collect the sediment around the base, with the tap above. The beer was duly brewed about a week before Christmas. Ideally it should have been brewed about a month before drinking but Woog always left it late. Dod tested it regularly and, after taking a sip, he would make a strange noise as he sucked in air through his teeth.His upper body would then shake in an uncontrollable fashion and he would declare, 'It's coming on well, but needs a bit longer.' The barrel would stand on a table in the hallway and – ready or not – come Christmas, any guests were offered a beer as they came in. Those who knew no better would accept. Bill Beaumont, at six foot six and known to be able to drink several gallons of beer in a session, was nearly rendered unconscious by it, and on another occasion Paul Frost (who lived only two hundred yards up the road) was found lying in our porch the next morning, cold but still alive.

The stage was now set for the great day. I could always tell it was Christmas Day as it was the only day of the year when little dishes of roasted peanuts were placed on the table in the front room. Dod always took Woog and myself to the morning service in the Cathedral. This was not our local church just down the hill but as Dod said, 'The music is better at the Cathedral.'

Then there were Dod's Christmas visits. He genuinely felt that if he did not go to all his local pubs and personally wish each landlord a Happy Christmas then they would at best be

44

upset, and at worst think he must have died. The first stop was usually the Crawshay Arms, followed by the Cat on the Barrel, the Whalebone at the bottom of the hill and a selection of others, usually ending up at the Constitution.

This little pub-crawl would ensure that Christmas lunch was ruined, but somehow Zomp always salvaged the situation and at about four in the afternoon we would all sit down to the festive repast. Christmas crackers and silly hats were of course mandatory. In later years Zompie introduced a new invention called the party popper. This technology proved too much for Dod, particularly at that late time of day. With his plastic red nose in place and a paper hat set at a jaunty angle, he let off the best part of a dozen party poppers, complaining that none of his had worked. It was only when a pile of paper streamers gradually became visible at table height that we realised he was letting them off upside down directly into his lap.

Christmas lunch was topped off with the traditional flaming of the Christmas pudding. In the early days, one of the Grannies would put a few sixpences inside. I am surprised this tradition was allowed to continue for as long as it did, since it was disastrous for the teeth and was it was only finally stopped when somebody swallowed one of these silver coins and had to have his stools examined for several few days before it was recovered. I am not sure what happened to it subsequently or if it was ever used again as currency. Every year Dod placed a small sprig of holly on the pudding, poured a liberal amount of brandy over it, set a match to it and found that nothing happened! This process would then be solemnly repeated until the whole half-bottle of brandy (bought specially for this purpose) had been used up. Then at the final attempt the pudding would catch fire and explode. How we laughed and clapped as bits of Christmas pudding flew across the room and Dod tried to extinguish his eyebrows. Once the pudding had been scraped off the walls and ceiling, Dod added

45

a large dollop of brandy butter to what remained, and it was distributed between us.

Then came the time to open our presents. No one could recall the exact origin of the Leaping Tiger, and of course *that* was the problem. Someone – who obviously had no taste – had given us this six-inch long ornament of yellow and black china, but no one could now remember who it was. Zompie was therefore insistent that we had to leave it out on show, just in case the person who had given it to us came round. It was quite ghastly and appeared sadly to be unbreakable. Many times I dropped it but it steadfastly refused to shatter. I think I was the first to receive the Leaping Tiger as a Christmas present. None of us had realised that in the weeks before Christmas it had disappeared from the mantelpiece. After all the presents had been opened, Zompie found this final one with my name on it. Excitedly I tore the wrapping paper off and could scarcely conceal my pleasure as the Leaping Tiger was revealed.

The following year I disguised it as a bottle and presented it to Woog. He similarly found it difficult to control his emotions and went pale with delight when he opened the parcel to find the Tiger was to be his for a whole year. This process then continued as the Tiger made its way round the family, year upon year. Indeed it sometimes surfaced at birthdays as well as at Christmas. I'm not sure what eventually happened to it, but even now, when I receive a present of a certain size and shape, I worry that it might be the Leaping Tiger come back to haunt me. And so, with more eating and drinking, the day would wear on towards its natural conclusion.

When older, Woog and I would usually walk down to the Elm Tavern, the only local pub open on Christmas Day evening, to have a couple of pints and then wander back. Dod would normally be asleep in his rocking chair in front of the fire, his mouth half open and looking festive with his plastic red nose now perched on his forehead, his paper hat at a rakish angle and streamers hanging down over his face while moving gently in and out with his breathing. Every now and again with a deeper breath the streamers would disappear into his mouth as he inhaled. He would then cough, splutter a bit and wave them away with a sweep of his arm, muttering half-asleep, 'Jolly good. . . jolly good day. Anyone for a Drambuie?' And then he would doze off once more.

CHAPTER 8: CHAIRMAN DOD

There can be no doubt that if Dod's hearing had been less impaired the whole political landscape of the U.K. from the 1960s onwards might have been entirely different. Lance-corporal Gunner Howard had been honourably discharged from the army in 1943 because of deafness. I would have thought that if your job was firing very loud guns, being deaf would have been a distinct advantage – but apparently not. You needed good hearing to be a gunner in the British army, presumably so that you could hear when someone told you to stop firing.

This deafness persisted throughout the rest of his life but seemed to vary, depending on the company he was in. His loss of hearing could be a real problem on his perennial visits to see the manager of Barclays Bank on St. Giles Street. Words like 'overdraft' and 'limit' were particularly difficult for him to hear, yet in the Victoria, a fine old pub next door to the bank, to where he would retire afterwards, his hearing would amazingly recover. In fact, the public house seemed to be an excellent hearing environment for him. 'What are you drinking, Bill?' was a phrase which obviously involved sound frequencies and wavelengths which had remained undamaged by the guns. Lucky that! Doctors have traditionally defined deafness as high-tone or low-tone. Clearly this dogma needs to be challenged and I prefer to use the Dod terminology of 'drinking-associated' or 'non-drinking-associated' deafness.

Dod was always a political animal. Broad-minded and fair in discussion, it wasn't that he was bigoted; it was simply that he disagreed with anyone and anything that was not true-blue Tory. He was apoplectic when I proudly showed him Harold Wilson's autograph which I had secured during a Scout camp in the Scilly Isles. Never a political commentator blessed with in-depth (or indeed any) knowledge, he never allowed political theory to get in the way of his own personal bias. By the standards of my aunt however, who wanted everyone who was not a Tory to be put up against a wall and shot, he was rather weak and leftish. My aunt also wanted to shoot all trade-unionists. Her husband, my uncle, an intelligent man, informed her that you could no longer do that sort of thing, so she settled for wanting to shoot half of them as long as that included 'that man Scargill!'

Dod was a regular attender at the Catton Ward Conservative Party meetings. These used to be held in some dingy church hall within Old Catton on the northern edge of Norwich. Traditionally Labour through and through, it was a pretty soul-destroying business being a Conservative in the north of Norwich. I am amazed that they bothered, but Dod diligently went canvassing before elections. He would don his blue rosette and knock on front doors, asking politely, 'Can we count on your vote in the forthcoming election (Sir or Madam)?' When the answer came back as an emphatic 'No', he would put that down as 'undecided'. Some kind souls would answer in the affirmative, but this was clearly just a ruse to get him off their doorstep, Needless to say, when the results of an election were at odds with Dod's canvassing experience, he would be astounded and customarily blame the weather on voting day.

It was at one AGM of the Catton Ward Conservative Party that the political landscape was affected by Dod's deafness. He always claimed he could hear someone who spoke clearly (such as our headmaster) but when someone mumbled (such as his bank manager) after a brief period of trying to follow the proceedings he would switch off, let his mind wander and gently doze. He would still nod at the right places, clap when necessary and smile benignly and knowingly throughout, while in fact being sound asleep. This coping mechanism worked well but was by no means foolproof, as was exemplified on one occasion by him enthusiastically breaking into loud applause in the middle of a particularly boring sermon in the school chapel.

It was at one such meeting that Dod agreed to become the chairman. Well, he didn't actually agree, but, after a determined though unsuccessful effort to keep up with the proceedings and stay awake, he had quietly dozed off at the back of the hall. The highlight of the political year arrived as the office holders were nominated, seconded and duly voted in. This was a time when it would have been wise for Dod to have stayed awake. I personally think it was slightly underhand to nominate someone who was quietly snoring in the back row but that is what happened. Dod was in that pleasant half-world – not hearing, but, at a kind of reflex level, still able to put his hand up and clap at the appropriate time. Not one to have strong opinions, his hand went up to support the nomination, first for treasurer and then for secretary. The final vote was for chairman. Having no idea what was going on, he raised his hand when everyone else did and so voted himself in as chairman of the Catton Ward Conservative Party.

It was only later, when a number of the attendees came up to congratulate him on his election and the newly-elected secretary announced that he was looking forward to working with him, that he realised something momentous had happened.

Dod's first action as chairman was a political masterstroke. He moved the venue for the meeting from the church hall to the Crawshay Arms, one of the many hostelries he frequented. This streamlined the political process enormously. Under the previous administration the meeting had to be declared closed before members of the Catton Ward Conservative party could have a drink. As the meeting often dragged on, this could at times come dangerously close to closing time. Now they could do both activities simultaneously. This was cutting-edge politics. As proceedings of the meetings were confidential and theoretically of national importance, the meeting had to held when the pub was quiet: this meant beginning as soon as the pub opened in the evening, a further advantage of Dod's procedural change. At that time of day, the only other incumbents of the bar were those who had never managed to leave at lunchtime and were therefore unlikely to follow the convoluted intricacies of Catton Ward's local politics. If anyone did show an unnatural interest in the proceedings they would be invited to join the Conservative party, which usually did the trick. It seemed that the Crawshay Arms was a safe house, albeit a public one. Even at the height of the Cold War, I do not recollect any unhealthy interest from Russian-speaking drinkers and the sales of Vodka did not increase. Meetings were held monthly but informal meetings, particularly those close to election time, were held more often, sometimes being so informal that Dod was the only person present. His dedication was never questioned.

For reasons I will never fully understand, an American student came to stay with us during one of those election campaigns. Presumably he was studying politics at some American university and had come across to see British politics at first hand during an election campaign. His name was Ben and he was massive. Some large men are surprisingly well coordinated and agile for their size. Not this one. His hands were huge, he was about six feet six tall, he must have weighed nearly 20 stone, and he was totally uncoordinated. He left a trail of destruction behind him – and a nicer man you couldn't hope to meet.

We witnessed the power of Ben's destructiveness at first hand when he pulled our bathroom wall down. He grabbed the towel rail as he stood up from the toilet (a procedure which had never before caused structural damage) and the towel rail, still attached to a large portion of the wall, came away in his hand. On another occasion he came in through the front door, apologetically holding the front door handle in his hand. I often wonder what opinion he took away of British politics, Catton Ward-style.

Voting day was a particularly busy day for the Catton Ward

Conservatives. The blue rosettes were donned after breakfast. There would be an initial political briefing and Dod, along with others, would go and pick up some old men and women who couldn't get out of the way in time, and take them to vote. I am sure most didn't want to go, and those who did voted Labour. Then there were those who took the opportunity to get a lift to the shops. At lunchtime there would be a briefing, sometimes lengthy, in the Crawshay Arms, which had become Tory party headquarters for the day, when everyone talked about the turnout and Dod said repeatedly, 'Everything seems to be was going jolly well.' Then would then be a final round-up of those who had previously resisted the invitation to vote. Further briefings began at about six in the evening and the Crawshay would be heaving by seven.

By this time, if you didn't want to vote, you were probably safe since by then no one was capable of driving. The results were then announced at the City Hall in the early hours of the morning. Special licensing hours allowed debriefing meetings to go on well into the following day, when Dod would thank his crew and blame the weather for the inevitable Labour victory.

The great British population of North Norwich had once again exercised their democratic rights. It would take a day or two to recover, and then the Catton Ward faithful would regroup and fight on under Dod's chairmanship. After numerous years as chairman and with as many election failures to his name, Dod eventually decided to stand down. As a reward for his services, he was elected Honorary President of the Catton Ward Conservative party, a post he held until he died.

CHAPTER 9: ZOMP'S PROGRESS

Dod was driving Woog and me home one Sunday after Matins when he said with a smile, 'Managed to avoid the Bursar today, boys', then adding, as he drew on his cigarette, 'Enjoyed the anthem, old boy – a bit flat on the high notes though'. This comment was directed at me, since I'd sung a duet that morning along with another treble. I really wanted praise, but Dod was right; and in fact was being generous, for it had not been a good performance.

'Yes, it was awful!' I replied. Woog agreed it had been awful, but as he was tone-deaf his comments didn't matter – though Dod's did. He had been a chorister and soloist as a boy; but more importantly, what hurt was the fact that he was correct. Nerves had got the better of me and the duet had gone from flat to sharp and back again with regularity during the performance.

Zomp was in the kitchen when we arrived home. 'How did it go, dear?' she asked.

'It was awful', I said, running upstairs to change out of my school uniform and into my play clothes.

Dod changed and went out to see his pals for a few beers while Woog and I played in the garden as Zomp prepared lunch. Sunday lunch was never actually ready: its status changed directly from being not quite ready to being ruined, usually because Dod was late. On this occasion Dod *was* late and it *was* ruined. As Dod returned smiling and smelling of beer, he gave Zomp a peck on the cheek. 'That was a beery kiss', she commented, then added, 'The dinner's ruined – you said you would be back at one'.

'Yes, sorry I'm a bit late but Ken insisted that we had a final pint as we were on an uneven number.'

'Well, you start carving and I'll dish up.'

Then I saw what I least wanted to see – sprouts. 'Not sprouts, Mum', I wailed. 'You know we hate sprouts.'

'You'll have them and like them,' said Dod.

'I've cooked those Norfolk puddings that old Thompson bought round,' Zomp continued.

The man Thompson had started to bring round some traditional Norfolk puddings. They were large white floury creations which we didn't particularly like, but Dod and Zomp were far too polite to say so. When asked if we had enjoyed them, Dod had said they were lovely, so Thompson now thought he was doing us a great favour in giving us those whenever he could get some. Thompson said that traditionally you ate them with gravy as a first course, presumably to fill you up so that you didn't need anything else.

'I hate sprouts,' I said again in case no one had heard the first time.

'I'll sprout you!' said Dod threateningly. I have never understood this type of humour but whenever Woog or I said something Dod didn't approve of he would turn it round in this fashion. Sunday lunch was a sombre affair with little conversation, particularly so if sprouts were involved. Looking up from her plate at Dod, Zomp remarked, 'Tommy's coming round to measure up this afternoon, dear,'

'What's he measuring up this time?'

'The back gate,' Zomp replied.

'I hope he does it quicker than the garage doors. That took forever. Eat your sprouts, Spoz,' said Dod, looking sternly at me again.

Having eaten the more pleasant parts of my lunch, I was now left with just six sprouts on my plate. While Woog, Zomp and Dod started on their pudding, I was left looking at my plate – forbidden to progress until it was empty. Pudding finished, the table was cleared, dishes washed and Woog went out for the afternoon. Dod and Zomp went next door to read the Sunday papers while I was left in the dining room in front of my plate of cold sprouts. In the winter I could put them on the fire when no

54

one was looking but in the summer disposal was more difficult. One way or another, I eventually cleared my plate. 'Finished, Mum,' I shouted.

'I'll finish you!' I heard from the front room.

On Sundays Dod took a hot bath. The rest of the week he had a cold bath in the morning but on Sundays we saved the hot water for his weekly soak and hair wash. As a boy I was always pleased when Sunday was over. As the last bars of 'Sing Something Simple' by the Adams Singers faded away and the wireless was switched off, I knew it would be a whole week before there would be another battle of wills over sprouts.

As we grew older, Sundays changed, ultimately for the better. Zompie was the first of us to learn to drive. She had had some professional lessons but needed driving experience and we would therefore go out for a drive most Sundays. These driving lessons were painful. Dod had never learned to drive, or rather had never taken a driving test, and he was not a patient man. The lesson would begin after the service in the school chapel. Woog and I piled into the back seat of the Morris Minor which we then had, while Dod climbed into the front passenger seat as Zomp adjusted the driving seat. Zomp always started the driving lesson with a plea: 'Now, Bill, don't shout at me. You know I'm just learning and shouting doesn't help.'

'Of course not,' he replied, already growing annoyed at Zompie's tone and the insinuation that he was anything other than a paragon of patience. Woog and I steeled ourselves for what we knew could only go badly. 'Right – mirror, indicate, manoeuvre,' Zomp announced, as much to herself as to Dod. With this, she let in the clutch and as the car leapt forward we were all thrown violently backwards into our seats. There followed a series of jerky movements as the car gained speed and as the engine screamed painfully in first gear Dod suggested that she consider changing to second. Looking down from the windscreen and grasping the long gear stick, Zomp took her eye off the road and in so doing turned the steering wheel to her left so that the car swerved violently toward the kerb. Dod grabbed the wheel and steered the car back toward the road, saying, 'Well done, that's fine,' with admirable self-control. Looking up again, Zomp sighed, 'I'll never get the hang of this', as she repeated the exercise to change into third and then fourth gear. By now we were travelling at a steady twenty-eight miles an hour down a straight road heading for Wroxham. We had all begun to relax a little when Zomp spotted a car about three miles away coming towards us in the opposite direction. 'Oh, Bill! There's a car. What do I do now?' she yelled.

'You're fine; just stay on your side of the road and there'll be no problem,' Dod reassured her. As the approaching car came nearer, Zompie steered closer and closer to the left-hand side of the road and slowed down to about twenty miles an hour. We were now on a slight upward incline and the engine was straining in fourth gear.

'I think you should change down a gear now, dear', suggested Dod. Zomp looked down, searching for the gear stick, and in doing so once again swerved to the left into the dried mud at the side of the road. She then alternated her glances between the road ahead and the gear stick. The car was now jerking along at about fifteen miles an hour but was still in fourth gear.

'Change down a gear! Change! Change!' Dod's voice was getting ever louder.

'I can't! It won't change' cried Zomp as expensive crunching noises came from under the bonnet each time she tried to engage a lower gear.

'Push the clutch in!' Dod shouted,

'Don't shout at me.'

'I am *not* shouting,' shouted Dod.

There followed more grating noises as Zomp finally engaged

second gear and we were all thrown forward when the car suddenly slowed. By this time there was a queue of cars behind us and some were sounding their horns.

'Right! That's it,' said Zompie as she steered the car to the side of the road where she neatly stalled it. 'You drive!' she yelled, getting out of the car and slamming the door behind her.

Back home in the safety of No. 3 and after a stiff gin and tonic, Dod ventured, 'I think you drove very well today, dear You just need a little bit more practice.' Woog and I agreed as we mutually vowed to be busy whenever the next lesson took place.

Amazingly, after a year or more of lessons, Zompie passed her driving test first time, and bought a small Simca. This gave her freedom and meant that she could now go to work. Her first job entailed travelling around the county auditing the sales of various goods in small corner shops. It was now 1973 – the year that saw the introduction of decimal currency. This was not popular in Norfolk and shopkeepers assured Zompie that it would never catch on. Her new-found freedom, however, meant Zompie could make friends outside Dod's circle of friends and for the first time in her married life she had an independent income. Pieces of new furniture began to appear in the house: first a three-piece suite for the front sitting room and then a stereogram. Until then we only had seventy-eights which were played on the wind-up gramophone. Now LPs began to appear – mainly Dod's personal favourites, including the soundtracks from *My Fair Lady* and *The King and I*, along with two Jack Buchanan albums.

Woog became less evident around the house, becoming a leading member of the local cactus society – then he began seeing girls. On occasion, Zomp invited her friends round when they would chat and drink a sherry or two. Cups of tea and rock buns were gradually replaced by gin and tonics and canapés.

As Zompie became busier, Thompson was enlisted to help with the housekeeping. His job was dusting and – like his measuring up – this took some considerable time. The difficulty was that he was short and suffered from ankylosing spondylosis which meant he was permanently bent over and unable to straighten or bend his back. His dusting was therefore limited to levels and surfaces which lay between two and four feet from the ground. In fairness I must say that this particular stratum of the house was kept dust-free.

Zompie also took up a hobby. She went to an evening class and learned how to paint porcelain. Dod was somewhat concerned about this new-found emancipation. Zomp tried to interest Dod in her hobby and spoke with admiration about her tutor who came round to visit on one occasion. He was good-looking, aged about forty, with a beard and longish hair. Dod was not impressed. 'Arty-farty sort! Never trust a man with a beard,' he said knowledgeably to Zomp. 'They always have something to hide.' Then he added, 'Of course, it's all right if you're in the Navy or have some facial deformity; otherwise it's a sure sign of a flawed character.'

Zomp was not convinced and continued to bring home very pretty porcelain tea and dinner services that she had painted.

As Zompie began to spread her wings, life also started to become more interesting for Woog and myself. Woog became something of a thespian, while I discovered sport, music and girls. We also began to develop our keen and enduring interest in pubs.

CHAPTER 10: ADOLESCENT AWAKENING

It is excruciatingly painful for a boy to be in an all-male environment when testosterone kicks in and adolescence starts. For one thing, at King Edward VI School long trousers could only be worn on entry to a certain year. I forget which it was but I do remember that because I was very tall for my age, this meant I was still wearing short trousers when I was almost six feet tall. Consequently I felt myself to be a figure of ridicule from the age of thirteen to about sixteen when things started looking up a bit. Access to the opposite sex was a particular problem for someone as shy and introverted as I was. Sport was one way to meet girls, but the lacrosse and hockey matches against the local girls' schools were for sixth-formers only. So I took up fencing. This, I felt, was cool and would give me a slightly piratical yet sophisticated air. I imagined saying to a wide eyed girl, 'Just going fencing. Would you like to come and watch?' And then I would energetically and athletically win my bout, watched adoringly by some girl who would later fall effortlessly into my arms. The trouble was that I had no one to hear this killer line. The real bonus of getting into the fencing team was that you might be selected to play St Felix School in Southwold. This was an all-girls school and was a splendid opportunity to meet girls off-limits. I was duly selected and indeed was vice-captain for the night. Full of eager anticipation, we were bussed to Southwold and the girls' school. After changing we were ushered into the school gymnasium where the girls' team, which had been ready for some time, was waiting and the two teams sat opposite one another at opposite ends of the gym; a harbinger of dull school dances in the future. The St. Felix fencing team were a gorgeous bunch, every single one of them. Of course they were – they were girls after all. There was, however, one particularly pretty girl who was also a good fencer. I suspect the boys didn't want to hurt her and consequently she kept winning her bouts. Eventually, it was my turn to play against her. With masks off, we raised our foils in the traditional pre-contest salute and I gave her my best smile. Being tall, I had a long reach and had developed a few competent fencing moves. I was absolutely determined to win. After a few moves I scored my first hit: a stylish lunge and my foil was arched with the button at its tip firmly into my opponent's jacket: so it was one-nil to me. Two more and I'd be home and dry and who knows – maybe a date would follow. After more fencing and several parried ripostes I scored another good hit and was two up. I could tell that she was growing annoyed. She had won all her bouts thus far and was about to lose for the first time that evening. Then came disaster. As I lunged once more, the tip of my foil made a tinny clanging sound as it bounced off her breast protection plate. I was mortified. I had hit her on the breast. I had indirectly touched a pretty girl's breast. I blushed behind my fencing mask and lost all concentration. My thoughts were now focused on breasts alone and on this girl's left breast in particular. She rapidly equalled the score and scored the winning hit before I could recover. As we took off our masks and saluted, I briefly looked her in the eye where I saw a defiant glare – and I'm certain she pushed her chest out as I walked off the piste. As I sat down on the bench next to the captain, he said, 'You were doing well there for a while, Grahame. Whatever happened?'

'Must have lost concentration,' I replied, as my mind reverted to that close encounter with the pretty girl's breast.

The dance hall, the 'Samson and Hercules', was on the west side of Tombland, opposite the Erpingham Gate which opened into the Cathedral Close. It was so named because it had a most imposing entrance with two larger-than-life statues, presumably of Samson and Hercules, holding up the roof of this porch-like structure. By now a venue for Bingo and discos, this was always where we held our school dance. By the time I started going to those dances I was a gangling youngster, six foot three, and with a prominant Adam's apple. As we spent most of our life in school uniform, neither Woog nor I possessed much in the way of casual wear and what we had was functional rather than stylish. On dance nights I duly put on my best clothes but it was difficult looking cool in cavalry twill trousers, a checked Viyella shirt, a Harris Tweed sports jacket, and – worst of all – a Paisley-pattern cravat. It was not surprising that I never pulled. Even if a girl took pity on me and was kind enough to dance, my jerky imitation of one of the Flower Pot men would ensure that she would never make that mistake again.

There were those who had girl friends and were reputed to have 'known' them, in the biblical sense. I felt my time would come eventually and that it was important to be prepared. I needed some condoms. The only problem was there was no way I could ask for these in a chemist's shop since I knew I would die with embarrassment. I couldn't countenance asking a pretty sales assistant (all women under the age of fifty being pretty) for a packet of condoms, since to buy a packet of Durex was tantamount to saying I wanted to have sex with them. A pub's male toilet was the only option. For months I would take every opportunity to pop into a pub for a half of bitter. Although well under age I was never challenged because I was so tall. Having taken my beer, I then went to the gent's to see if there was a condom machine. Every time I went in, there either was someone already there or, just as I was about to put the coins in the machine, the toilet door would open and someone would enter. I simply couldn't let anyone see me obtain those items, being bizarrely convinced that somehow the whole world would find out. After many months of trying, and many halves of beer, I finally managed to buy a packet of three. I placed them ready for instant action in my wallet where they remained untouched for several years. Eventually they moulded an oval visibly condom-shaped contour in the leather of my wallet which could be seen every time I opened it.

As friends and colleagues reached the age of sixteen, wheels began to appear on the scene. To be mobile was again cool and significantly increased one's pulling power. Different modes of transport clearly offered differing degrees of attractiveness to the opposite sex. At the top end of the spectrum was a proper car – that is, one with four wheels, doors which opened and which reliably worked. Some of the older boys were lucky enough to have access to one. Thus, Pete Stringer was cool. He had helicopter-pilot dark glasses and a car. The only problem was that his vehicle was of the three-wheel variety – a Reliant Robin. Pete had adjusted the seat so that his arms had to be held straight out to reach the steering wheel, just like Steve McQueen in *Bullitt*, but even with a re-spray *and* wearing dark glasses this was never going to have the pulling power of his hero's Mustang. One farmer's son had a green Morris Minor van which smelt of manure. He didn't seem at all embarrassed by this. I asked him how fast it went and he responded in a broad Norfolk accent, 'That's got a bit of poke', meaning (I think) that it went fairly fast. For the rest of us, it was bikes, and my pedal cycle in due course was replaced by a BSA Bantam 175. This ancient motorcycle cost me £25 and was very unreliable. It is probably fair to say that I walked with it as often as I rode on it.

I could now ride to the Folk Club and to dances. I swapped the tweed jacket for an old army surplus khaki tunic, exchanged the cavalry twill for Levis and the cravat for a red silk kerchief. I was not altogether cool but it was a distinct improvement. School dances and rock concerts remained the staple dating diet. One Saturday evening, Mike and I rode our bikes to a school on the south side of Norwich where a band was performing. The concert was in the gymnasium which was half full of teenagers and where an amateurish rock band was loudly doing its stuff on stage. As I went out for a smoke with Mike, a complete stranger approached and asked if we were the boys with the motorbikes. Proudly we acknowledged the fact.

'Well,' said the stranger, 'The band would like a bit of action on stage. Would you be able to ride your bikes around the stage a bit while they play?' This seemed an entirely reasonable suggestion to us, and had the potential for quite a lot of fun. Mike and I looked at each other and, without giving further thought as to whether it was really a very good idea, replied, 'Yeah, why not?'

We tied our scarves across the lower half of our faces, put on our helmets and placed goggles over our eyes. As soon as the band started the second half of the concert, we rode into the gymnasium revving the engines very loudly. I think it's fair to say there was a mixed reaction to our entrance. Some clapped; some shouted abuse; but all were taken by surprise. We were directed toward the stage by the stranger who had approached us outside. The three steps up to the stage were difficult to negotiate but we managed and eventually rode round the stage, still revving noisily while our bikes belched out thick clouds of exhaust fumes. Rather to our surprise, the band members did not seem entirely pleased to see us and in retrospect I suspect we had been set up. After a short time someone yelled to us that the police had been called and Mike and I felt that it would be an appropriate time to leave. Down the steps we drove, through the gymnasium, out into the playground and straight on to the road. We didn't stop till we got home. I spent an anxious weekend, constantly expecting the police to knock at the front door at any moment. Surreptitiously phoning Mike, we agreed to do nothing but keep our heads down for the rest of the weekend. On Monday, the word was out at school that two idiots had driven their motorbikes on to the stage at a concert and it had been ruined. The police had been called and there was damage to the stage. Mike and I kept silent on the matter and amazingly our identities remained undisclosed.

By the age of seventeen I wanted to learn to drive and driving lessons were accordingly re-instigated. These were similar to Zompie's but involved beer. As before, lessons would normally take place on a Sunday. They began at about eleven-thirty and involved my driving Dod and Woog to the pub. To be fair to Dod, we did travel to pubs a bit further away than normal in order to enhance the driving experience. We then drank five or six pints before I drove the car back home. On arrival, Dod would invariably announce to Zomp,

'Spoz is driving very well, dear.'

'The dinner's ruined,' would come the inevitable reply.

'Time for a g and t, dear?' would be Dod's response as he started to pour them out.

'Well, it's already ruined, so I don't suppose a few more minutes will make any difference.'

We then drank a great deal of gin until about four o'clock when we eventually sat down to lunch. With admirable tuition like this I was both surprised and disappointed when I failed my driving test.

Being five years older than me, good-looking and urbane, Woog had a much wider and more interesting circle of friends than me. He soon became a popular man about town. He was in demand for parties and had an extensive collection of pretty girlfriends. He took care of his appearance and varied his style from trendy bohemian to Norfolk gentleman. He had a Norfolk jacket made for him. This was a belted tweed jacket with two breast and two side patch pockets. As Woog said himself, it was ideal for 'huntin', shootin' and fishin' but Woog was essentially a townie. Nonetheless he strode about Norwich as though he were a county landowner who was visiting town to shop.

Norwich was reputed to be blessed with 365 pubs, one for

each day of the year. Woog and I frequented as many of these as we could, to socialise and to play darts. Most had jukeboxes but some still had live music. There was Terry LaRoche (I suspect not his real name) the camp organist and singer in the Crawshay Arms and then there was the amazing one-armed pianist in the Angel Gardens. Well he wasn't really amazing but he really did only have one arm as the left had been amputated above the elbow. He used this stump to bash the bass keys while playing some unrecognisable tune with his right hand. After the First World War there were several one-armed classical pianists and some wonderful music had been written for them. This man, however, was not one of these, and the overall effect was a musical disaster. The Howards were generous with their patronage, but of all the many pubs we frequented the Constitution was undoubtedly our true local.

CHAPTER 11: THE CONSTITUTION

The Constitution was not some sort of formal documentation about the administration of the Howard household but rather the name of our nearest pub. Presumably it was so named because of its situation at the top of Constitution Hill, but the picture on the swinging sign outside was of some rather austere puritanical chaps dressed in black and white and solemnly signing a document. I have always presumed it was the American Constitution – but who cares?

The Constitution Tavern was on the opposite side of the road from our house and about a hundred yards to the right. When we first moved into No. 3, the pub was a dour, dark place with three bars, a lounge bar, a public bar and a jug bar, each accessed from a separate outside door. You got the same drinks in all three bars, but at different prices. The lounge bar was the most expensive, but had a carpet, a small glass container on the bar with an old sandwich in it and, occasionally, a real female customer. The public bar had plain floorboards and a jukebox. Most men drank mild beer there, and no woman had ever been seen within its confines. The jug bar was small and cramped, being intended for off-sales, but it could accommodate a small party of drinkers and no women would want to go in there. Even at peak hours there would only be a handful of customers in the pub – men in flat caps, mainly in the public bar. The landlord was a surly character who would serve you only if he wished to do so. The jukebox in the public bar was old, with hits from the fifties on it. On one occasion, while enjoying a quiet pint, Dod commented to the landlord, 'My word! That's a bit of an antique.'

Dod was taken aback by the angry response. 'If you don't like my jukebox you can drink elsewhere'. Dod retracted the accusation with his customary aplomb and all was well – but I think it was the closest that Dod ever came to being barred from a pub. He was always a well-behaved drinker and far too valuable a customer to ban.

Then Ronnie took The Constitution over. A retired Liverpudlian policeman, he renovated the pub, converting the three bars into one large one. He got rid of the jukebox, installed piped music, and covered the new long bar with polished old penny coins. There was an article about the makeover in the *Eastern Evening News*, together with a picture of Ronnie standing behind the coin bar. He also began to serve hot food. This period of pub grub and Watney's Ales was not however a high point for lovers of good food and fine ale. The beer was of a diuretic nature and so weak that you needed about ten quick pints to get a lift of any sort, by which time the drinker was completely water-logged. It was said that that the Norfolk and Norwich Constabulary never bothered to breathalyse anyone who had been drinking Watney's Starlight as it was believed impossible to drink enough of the stuff to be over the driving limit. The food served comprised deep-fried chicken or fish, both with chips – which probably accounts for the high incidence of coronary heart disease ten years later. For reasons I have never understood, the meal was always served in a basket. Indeed, if you go to Norfolk now there are still some pubs that serve food in a basket rather than on the more traditional plate. Having said that, there remain some pubs in Norfolk where the cigarette machines still take pre-decimal coins – and, more worryingly, some customers still have currency to use in them.

I have never understood why serving food in a basket proved so popular when plates have such clear advantages. Obviously soup couldn't be served in a basket, although I suspect some Norfolk landlords might have conceivably tried to do so; but all other meals were served up in a wicker basket. This was supposed, I imagine, to make the whole dining experience much more sophisticated. Indeed, if you wanted to impress a girlfriend, you wouldn't just ask her out for dinner, but rather would say,

'Would you like to come out for a meal *in a basket*?' With an opener like that, you were already half way there – that is, if the resulting indigestion didn't incapacitate you first.

The Constitution suddenly became *the* place to go. Rather than one or two old men in flat caps drinking mild, playing shove ha'penny and listening to Al Martino, it was now packed. The car park was full, the bar was busy, and there were more pictures of the coin bar in the *Eastern Evening News*. With some skilled marketing, Ronnie had turned it into a popular meeting-place for young and old alike, while women, especially young pretty ones, were welcome.

Dod, Woog and I used to drink there a lot, and we used to drink a lot there.

Woog and I would often go for an early ale and a game of darts at about six o clock. On most days the bar was pleasantly quiet at that time, and on one particular occasion the only other customer was seated at the opposite end of the bar. He was a middle-aged man perched precariously on the edge of a tall bar stool, his head upon his arms which in turn rested on the coin bar. In front of him was a pint glass three-quarters full. He would occasionally awake briefly from his stupor but after an incoherent word or two would lapse back into semi-consciousness. Woog and I chuckled and agreed that this was someone who had clearly peaked far too early.

About half an hour later, Dod arrived. When we pointed out the state of the unfortunate drinker, the man looked blearily at Dod and tried to raise one hand in salute.

'Hello, Pat. How are you?' said Dod cheerily as he ordered a round of drinks. 'Three pints please, Ronnie; Oh, and one for Pat, please.'

In an attempt to thank Dod, Pat endeavoured to raise his head and his hand simultaneously, an action which so destabilised him that he fell completely off his bar stool. After we had lifted him from the floor and seated him safely at a table, Dod remarked to Ronnie, 'It might be best if you to kept that one in salt for Pat.'

To the serious drinker like Dod, drinking was akin to an art form. Different pubs opened and closed at different times. There were Market licensing hours in the centre of Norwich, which meant that on a Saturday you could drink the whole day through, as long as you were bone-fide market traders, which of course we were. Suffolk licensing hours were different and closing time was half an hour later than in Norfolk, being at ten-thirty. Dod would therefore often aim to end up at a hostelry near the border so that he had the opportunity of popping across the border for a final one or two in Suffolk.

Then Ronnie put his prices up – and Dod was appalled! He confidently predicted that custom would fall off and each time he went in he would comment loudly that it was much quieter and that the car park was half-empty. He even threatened not to go there. No one else noticed any difference and Ronnie made enough profit to sell up and move to the States with a regular called Mr Bastard. He really was called that and, if you tried to soften the blow by calling him Mr B'Stard or something sounding slightly different, he would correct you and loudly insist you called him Bastard. 'Bastard by name and bastard by nature,' he would add. He was very wealthy and had both a Mercedes (at a time when most people had only seen them in films) as well as a Ford GT 40.

Dod treated the landlords of his many locals as friends of the family. He considered it rude not to visit them on a regular basis – just as you would a relative.

'We really should go and see Jimmy soon, dear. We haven't been for far too long. He'll wonder what has happened to us,' Dod would say to Zomp as the weekend approached.

At Christmas this created significant problems since every landlord required a visit on Christmas Day, I really believe Dod felt they would be offended if we didn't go. This inevitably led to severe beer-overloading prior to our Christmas lunch which (as the reader will remember) would follow at about four in the afternoon. On reflection, this was much the same as any Sunday really.

Woog and I, together with our groups of friends, trod a fine line between acceptable youthful over-exuberance, and being banned from the Constitution. A core group of us used to meet there and, in fairness, tried to avoid being seen there (or at least misbehaving) when Dod and Zomp were present. Bruce, Mike, David, Andy and myself on an evening out would often start out from, or finish up at, the 'Conny'.

As I recall, it was Bruce's idea to blow up a condom in the main bar. It was usually his idea to do something stupid, like asking a tourist in Soho, 'How much?' in the mistaken belief that she was a prostitute. In a rowdy student-bar setting, blowing up a condom would have been entirely unexceptional. This, however, was nine o'clock in the evening on a Saturday night, and the bar was packed with Norwich's middle class – the men in their weekend suits, and their wives fresh from the hairdresser in their best frocks – all congregated there for their weekly treat of chicken and chips in a basket. It was standing-room only when this massive, air-filled rubber sausage began to push its way between the customers. My memory of the whole event remains vague, but I do recall Dod tut-tutting and Zompie howling with laughter while trying not to open her mouth so wide as to display her missing tooth. As the slimy balloon came close to them, customers screamed and tried to escape before being engulfed by this ghostly metamorphosing dirigible. Some ran for the safety of the car park, leaving half-drunk port and lemons, and half-devoured meals in baskets. I am still amazed at how enormous a condom can become when blown up – and this one seemed to fill the whole room. With remarkable composure under the circumstances, Ronnie politely told us to deflate what could now be described as a small dirigible; and so, in a final act of defiance, Bruce let the air out with an almighty farting sound. Dod and Zomp were never heard to mention the episode again.

CHAPTER 12: TURKEY PLUCKING

In my later years at school, money was always short. By then I had beer, cigarettes and petrol to buy, with no income apart from my pocket money. It was proving difficult to maintain credibility with girls when I had to admit half-way through a date that I'd run out of pocket money. Christmas was the best time to earn some extra cash. Most of us would enlist with the post office to do the pre-Christmas deliveries. If you got a delivery round on Christmas Eve this sometimes produced a few tips – which annoyed the regular postmen hugely. John, one of my pals from school, had a Christmas card returned to him with 'deceased' written on the outside. He opened it out of interest; inside was written, 'Hope you are keeping well. Love, Maisie.'

Turkey-plucking was a job I only tried once. As usual with idiotic ideas, it was one of Bruce's. He saw an advertisement in the *Eastern Evening News* seeking turkey-pluckers at what seemed like good rates of pay. A shilling per bird seemed like easy money and with Christmas just two weeks away this was clearly the solution to our financial problems. The barn where the turkey-plucking took place was out in the country, about fifteen miles from Norwich, but luckily my motor bike was working and Bruce's 50 c.c. moped also worked, provided he kept the throttle cable in a certain position with a mole wrench which dangled over the handlebars. We set off quite early in the morning, but lost our way and didn't find the barn until about eleven o'clock. Inside were dozens of people, mainly women, who had been there since sunrise and were by now ankle-deep in turkey feathers. The noise was deafening, with chattering, screeching women competing against hundreds of squawking turkeys. We went up to the surly-looking gaffer and asked if we could be taken on for the day.

'Have you done this before?' he asked suspiciously.

'No, never,' we admitted. 'But we're keen to learn,' we added, hoping this might make all the difference. The man sighed and said, 'All right, I'll show you what to do. 'First you have to catch a bird,' he said, walking towards a pen with about a dozen turkeys in it. Expertly, he threw his arms over the back of one to stop its wings from flapping. 'Mind the wings,' he warned. 'These can cause damage, so watch your eyes. Then grab the legs and hang them upside down from one of the beams,' he added, slipping a string noose round the turkey's legs. He stood back to admire his handiwork and looked at us. 'OK so far?' he asked. Bruce confessed that he hadn't realised we actually had to catch the turkey first, again emphasising (albeit somewhat less convincingly now) that we were keen to learn.

'Now for the hard part,' said the man, who now seemed to be rather enjoying himself, 'That's breaking its neck. Grab the neck firmly below the head and pull quickly downwards. You'll feel a crack when it's broken.' So saying, he neatly despatched the bird. 'Now start with the wing feathers,' he said, demonstrating how to pluck the bird until it was ready to hand in and earn us our shilling. The women were catching, killing and plucking a bird about once every ten minutes, while keeping up with the gossip at the same time.

By now I was not at all sure that this had been a good idea and Bruce himself looked a trifle pale. It was extremely cold in the barn and we were not really dressed for what in effect was an outdoor job in midwinter. We tossed a coin to see who would try first, I won and invited Bruce to catch his first turkey. After a moment's hesitation he said, 'Right! Let's do it' and climbed into the pen. Whatever people say, turkeys are not stupid birds and unsurprisingly when they saw Bruce approaching them with his arms wide and a determined look in his eye, they all ran to the far side of the enclosure. After a few failed lunges, Bruce managed to half-grab one. 'Got you!' he shouted triumphantly, just as he lost control of one of the wings which whacked him a glancing blow on the left cheek. It was at exactly that moment that the turkey decided to open its bowels on Bruce's jumper. On seeing this, Bruce lost his presence of mind and loosened his grasp, whereupon the bird escaped and half-ran, half-flew away.

Eventually, and with a few minor injuries, Bruce was able to get a turkey hung from a beam ready for the coup-de-grâce. Meanwhile, I had done the same and had a bird hanging nearby. Bruce grabbed the neck and pulled down. I watched with interest as the bird's neck seemed to stretch to twice its normal length, Bruce jumped back. 'Ugh! Its head nearly came off.' The bird was not only still alive but was growing increasingly annoyed. The man came over and in a resigned fashion despatched both birds expertly for us. 'You need to bend the neck, and then pull sharply,' he explained, 'The head won't come off,' he added reassuringly. We started plucking. The trick was to remove all the feathers without damaging the skin and this was not as easy it looked – big scars appearing in the flesh every time I pulled a feather out. Three quarters of an hour later, we handed in our two plucked birds. They looked as though they had been in a brawl, as indeed they had. The man was not impressed but marked our cards and we went off to repeat the process. The second attempt was no easier and after about two hours we had earned the princely sum of two shillings each. This was not proving to be the money-spinning venture we thought it would be. The final straw came when, as the next bird was hanging ready for despatching, Bruce grabbed its neck and pulled its head back and down energetically in the prescribed fashion, but unfortunately with such vigour that the string broke. The bird crashed to the floor and unsurprisingly was clearly upset and not a little angry. Quite reasonably, it decided to attack Bruce. Both of us were now liberally covered in turkey poo to which stray feathers had adhered, and Bruce was being viciously assaulted by a turkey with attitude. My friend was obviously finding the whole experience quite unsettling. *'That's it!'* he said finally. I agreed, and without hesitation we went to collect our two shillings.

'Will we be seeing you again?' said the gaffer with a smile.

'Unlikely,' replied Bruce, with what I thought was remarkable restraint under the circumstances.

The day finished off appropriately enough when just two miles down the road Bruce's mole wrench fell off and the engine gave a cough and died on him. Despite our best attempts we couldn't entice it to start again and found ourselves on the side of a narrow country road, somewhere in the middle of nowhere. Moreover it was beginning to get dark. Bruce suggested holding on to the back of my bike and being towed. This was another incredibly stupid idea. However after falling over a few times I found a short piece of rope which did the trick. In due course, frozen and covered in bird-shit and feathers, we arrived back at Bruce's house. His mother was in the kitchen facing away from us. 'Did you have a good day?' she asked brightly as we entered.

'Not very', Bruce replied grimly. Mrs Smithers then turned round and nearly fainted as she beheld the two apparitions standing in the doorway.

The two shillings had just about paid for enough petrol to get us to the barn and back. All in all, it wasn't a successful day's work. Bruce and I agreed not to attempt this particular money making scheme again. The post office was warmer and safer.

CHAPTER 13: DOD THE ENTREPRENEUR

After Dod's move from London to Norwich his networking began anew with a whole new bunch of colleagues. Once again he was unwilling to test the theory that business could be done by staying in the office – and so it was fieldwork, fieldwork, and yet more fieldwork. The days were long. After a brief visit to the office to check the mail, there was the morning's networking to attend to. This might involve upwards of five hostelries in and around town; hence a fast car was essential and an Austin A30 with a top speed of 55 m.p.h. downhill was just the job.

It was only a matter of time, Dod said confidently, before the business would come rolling in. Amazingly it did not. There were even some colleagues who had the audacity to suggest that networking was not the best way to get business and that more time in the office might help. This was sheer management-theory gobbledegook to a man still in an Edwardian time warp and proud of the fact that he had never been on a management course in his life. There was only one thing to do – resign. Dod didn't actually *mean* to resign, but he *offered* his resignation, and to his surprise it was promptly accepted. A dozen cut-glass whisky tumblers accompanied the event and he found himself unemployed.

When the going gets tough, as they say, the tough get going and Dod did what all like-minded men in this position would do. With some rather dodgy pals, he opened a shop to repair musical instruments. A departure from insurance certainly, but this was cutting-edge entrepreneurship. Business was slow to pick up – in fact so slow that it never did. Obviously there were not enough broken musical instruments in Norwich. He had misjudged the market and had made the fatal mistake of not networking enough.

Not at all deterred by this experience, Dod then joined a wholly new group of dodgy pals and became director of a

Norfolk Broads boat-building firm. He did not allow the complete absence of any experience whatsoever in the building or selling of boats to deter him. Given a significant investment, enormous financial rewards were as good as in the bank. Dod networked tirelessly, often to the detriment of his health. Sometimes he networked late into the night and could hardly walk when he got home. Mobility was essential and for some the combination of networking and driving might have been a problem. Not so for Dod. As luck would have it, he actually drove better 'after a few' as he was then more relaxed. This was fortunate. Sometimes he was so relaxed that he was sick but it is reassuring to know that he was still able to drive really well. Bankruptcy followed. It was becoming clear to us all that Dod's business fingers were not as green as he thought and so he returned to a salaried job, this time with Boulton and Paul and back to what he knew best – marine insurance.

As a younger man Dod had enjoyed rude health. Even forty cigarettes and numerous beers each day had not adversely affected his well-being. The first sign of the Dod's lifestyle catching up with him was when he was in his fifties and I was a junior doctor at home for a brief visit. One morning he came downstairs and walked into the kitchen complaining that his hands were shaking. As it happens, so were mine, since we had had a few in the Constitution the night before. Dod however looked very pale and later admitted to passing jet-black stools, something which he had failed to recognise as being of any significance. I drove him to the surgery and watched the goldfish (or was it guppies?) with mild interest as I waited for him to be seen. It was not long before I was asked to take him directly to the West Norwich Hospital (where he was later admitted with a suspected gastro-intestinal bleed) and told that he mustn't eat in case he needed an operation. I later learned his haemoglobin was just over forty grams per litre, about a quarter of what the level should be and only just compatible with life. We left the surgery and headed for the car, which was parked outside the Eagle, a pleasant hostelry which we sometimes frequented.

'Fancy a quick one before we go to the hospital? The doctor didn't say anything about not drinking,' Dod said. Unusually my sense of humour failed at that point and I escorted him firmly to the car. We visited that evening to find Dod sitting up in bed looking a lot better, having had a pint or two – 'Sadly of blood, not beer,' he said. 'The surgeon says that my duodenum looks like a scene from the First World War. Apparently there are craters everywhere,' Dod said proudly, rather pleased by the fact that his upper bowel resembled the Battle of the Somme. Amazingly, there was a return to full health and, even more amazingly, to full drinking capacity. Later came a change to pipe-smoking, but otherwise no real change in Dod's lifestyle. He treated his body more like a bonded warehouse than a temple.

CHAPTER 14: DOD'S TRAVELS

Some years later, after Woog and I had left home, we met up as a family in Wallasey to attend my cousin Carol's wedding. We had travelled up the day before and stayed separately with various relatives. We met on the day of the wedding at the Grove House Hotel where Dod and Zomp were staying, and from where Dod was to drive us all to the church. I had never before seen Dod use a map. Like a migrating bird, he seemed to trust to instinct and would rely on recognising buildings (usually pubs) to navigate.

'Ah yes! I know where we are now, dear. There's the Red Lion,' he'd say; or, 'I recognise the name of that street, I'm sure we're close by now.'

In retrospect, I'm amazed that we ever arrived at any destination when Dod was driving. Of course in those days if you were lost (or 'off track' as Dod preferred to call it) you would just stop and ask a policeman. While taking us to see his brother Ken, Dod once found himself a little off track. He pulled up alongside a bobby on the beat, narrowly avoiding driving over his toes, then wound down the window and said, 'Excuse me, officer, but I think we're a little off track. We're looking for my brother Ken's house.'

'Could you be a bit more specific, sir?' came the reply.

'Well, he's about six foot two, well-built, with black hair and glasses, and usually smokes a pipe,' Dod offered helpfully.

'I meant about where he might live, sir,'

'Oh yes, of course, officer, It's Green Bank or Green Lane or something like that,' and then, after a pause, adding, 'There's a bank on the corner and a Co-op close by.'

Amazingly, if we were within a ten mile radius of our destination, this would often be enough to get directions – assuming of course that the destination was the correct one in the first place. On the day of the wedding, Dod knew the name of the road, and also the fact that the ceremony was to be held in a Catholic church. Two such items of data should have been ample and this was one more than he usually had, but Dod made the fatal assumption that there was only one Catholic church on the road.

I think we should have smelt a rat when, at ten minutes before the time of the bride's arrival, we were the only people in full morning dress in the church. In fact we were the only people in the church, apart from a cleaner. Once she had informed us that there was another Catholic church down the road about four miles away, there was a somewhat undignified rush back to the car, with Zomp holding on to her hat with one hand and grasping her handbag with the other. Dod pretended that this was no more than a slight setback, saying, 'Don't worry, dear, we've plenty of time to get there,' adding rather unnecessarily, 'What a *glorious* day!'

We were still not altogether sure about the location of the correct church and were driving quite slowly down the road looking for a church or a policeman, whichever came first, when a wedding car passed us with ribbons fluttering and with a bride in the back.

'There she is, dear!' exclaimed Dod, as though this was exactly what he had been waiting for. 'We'll just follow that car.'

This strategy was of course not without risk, as it was unlikely that Carol's would be the only wedding on this sunny Saturday morning. From a distance, bridal limousines – and indeed brides – can look similar, but this was all or nothing. Dod had made his decision and this was the wedding we were going to, whoever's wedding it was.

The bridal car drew up slowly outside a church and once we had confirmed that this was its destination and that the bride did indeed look a bit like Carol, Dod accelerated hard, overtook the limousine, swerved deftly to avoid hitting the driver who was just getting out, and muttered, 'Damn fool: should have looked!' before coming to an abrupt halt about ten yards in front. We piled out of our car and were walking briskly into the church just as the organist pulled out the stops and let loose the first booming notes of Mendelssohn's Wedding March. As is always the case, the congregation turned round expecting to get their first glimpse of the bride. Instead, there was Dod, strolling casually through the entrance, smiling graciously, nodding to right and left, and wondering what all the fuss was about.

Into old age he would still navigate by pubs, or follow someone. This latter technique could be disastrous, as exemplified by one unfortunate occasion when he agreed to follow a friend back from a pub in Lowerstoft for a drink at his house. Mile after mile he followed his friend's car and Dod began to think that he was going rather a long way round when eventually the car turned into a drive and in the belief that they had finally reached their destination Dod followed the car into the drive, pulling up with a flourish behind it. With a big smile, Dod opened his door and was getting out of the car when he was met by a complete stranger who angrily asked him why he had been following him.

It was a characteristic of Dod that he could never disagree with anyone. Whatever their viewpoint or opinion, he would nod sagely and agree. If a contrary opinion was voiced by someone else he would nod and solemnly agree with them as well. This was where his deafness helped, as he could usually agree with several quite contradictory points of view at the same time. If really stuck, he would say, 'Awfully sorry, must have misheard you. My round! Same again everyone?' This inability to disagree, or to correct someone who was misinformed, could at times result in unfortunate situations.

Mrs Forman's in Musselburgh, outside Edinburgh, is not the most salubrious pub but it was just round the corner from where I was living at the time, having moved there to work in Edinburgh.

Dod and Zomp occasionally came to stay and one lunchtime Dod found himself in Mrs Forman's having a quiet pint, smoking his pipe and minding his own business. He was nearly four hundred miles from home and hardly expected his ruminations to be interrupted by anyone. In retrospect (the retrospectoscope being the most perfect of all optical instruments) it might have been better if he had not been wearing the blue jumper with canvas patches over the shoulders and elbows. Although from Marks and Spencer, it did look distinctly naval and Dod, with thick grey-to-white hair and smoking a pipe, did look rather nautical. Nonetheless it came as a complete surprise when a man, stockily-built and with a broad Scottish accent, came over to him and said,

'Twas a pleasure to serve under you, sorr!'

Dod was caught off guard. He had only heard half of the remark, and what he had heard he did not fully understand. 'I beg your pardon. I didn't quite catch what you said,' he said smiling politely,

'It was a pleasure' (and now the man became a bit more expansive) 'and a privilege to serve under you at sea, sorr,'

It now began to dawn on Dod that this was a major case of mistaken identity with potentially serious consequences and he started to try to correct the situation. He planned to say, 'It's nice to meet you, but I think you must be mistaken, as I have never been in the Navy, let alone commanded a ship.' Dod got only as far as, 'It's nice to meet you.' but that was ample comfirmation for Bob McTavish, ex-Royal Navy, (as this stranger turned out to be) that Dod was indeed Captain Beaufort of HMS Reliant.

By now Dod had been bought a pint and was being introduced to all in the bar the as 'the Captain'. What was more, it transpired that HMS Reliant had been sunk towards the end of the War. Clearly the Captain and McTavish had survived but many lives had been lost. Many more would have perished, it appeared, had it not been for the extraordinary seamanship of Captain Dod.

Things were now getting slightly out of hand. Everyone was getting in on the glory. With each round there would be added, 'And a pint for the Captain!' Dod had to reciprocate by ordering drinks for all his old shipmates and their friends; while everyone was shaking his hand and saying what a good chap he was. He was now in a slightly difficult position – to admit that the only ship he had ever commanded was a toy yacht on New Brighton boating pond would almost certainly lead to accusations of impersonating a captain of the Royal Navy and thereby acquiring free drinks under false pretences. Moreover, he was now having to dodge awkward questions about the Navy, warships, guns, and all manner of things maritime. The nearest Dod had got to the war was Catterick and that was nowhere near the sea.

Eventually, with a great nautical flourish, Dod extricated himself by muttering that it was ten bells o'clock, that the sun was now well over the yardarm and it that was time for him to go ashore. And so, amid laughter and applause, he left. Of course he could never go into Mrs Forman's again and for a while it was fairly dangerous even to be seen out and about in the vicinity. In the years that followed, as he strolled round Musselburgh occasionally, some elderly gentleman would salute him and Dod would respond with a relaxed wave and a benign smile.

CHAPTER 15: ZOMP'S DIET AND DECLINE

Zompie was forever on a diet. I cannot remember her ever not being on one. She owned the classical pear-shaped British figure which became more pear, and less shaped, as she grew older. Woog called her 'Football knees', which was unkind, despite being a reasonably accurate description of this region of her anatomy. Although Zompie was always on a diet I don't think she ever really dieted. She loved cream cakes and sweets so much that these seemed to be part of her diets. I was probably unwittingly responsible for this since on one occasion I jokingly said to her, 'I've found a cream-cake diet, Zomp. I thought you might be interested in it.'

'Oh, yes, dear,' she replied, unexpectedly taking me seriously. 'I'd like to try that one.' She never really stopped believing in the cream-cake diet and often said, while tucking into something nice at tea-time, that it was part of a diet I had discovered. One of Zomp's friends told her that she'd been given a tablet to help her diet. Zomp naturally asked her own doctor if she might have some, but he refused to prescribe them, even though she explained that they'd worked wonders for her pal, Mary. So Mary, bless her, gave Zomp one of her own tablets. It was called Tenuate Dospan and was meant to be part of a three-month course of treatment. This solitary tablet in its foil wrapping sat on the side table in the kitchen along with other kitchen detritus, such as pieces of string used for hanging the electric frying pan in the back toilet, and old newspaper articles which had been ripped out and kept, to be read at some time in the future because they looked potentially interesting. The tablet remained there half-buried for several years. Once I asked Zomp, 'Why don't you take the tablet?'

'I'm keeping it for a special occasion,' she retorted as though only an idiot would ask such a stupid question.

Eventually I tried to introduce some science into her dieting.

I drew a graph. On the vertical axis was her weight in stones and pounds while along the bottom was the time measured in weeks – to a total of twelve to match her three-month diet plan. This piece of graph paper was backed with cardboard and hung from the back-kitchen door by a piece of string. It was visible every time you opened the back door and hence could not be ignored. Things went swimmingly to start with as she lost about half a stone in the first week and a similar amount the week after. The graph plummeted to such a degree that I began to wonder about the accuracy of her scales. Then, noticing that the graph had not been filled in for some time I challenged Zomp: 'You haven't filled in your weight for the last three weeks?'

'Oh haven't I?' she responded innocently. When pressed for an explanation, she admitted that she only filled it in when she had lost weight, not if she had gained any. I carefully explained the flaw in this approach but she persevered with her policy, resulting in very few (if indeed any) points being added to the graph. The chart continued to hang on the door until she died some ten years later. Only when she was in the terminal phase of breast cancer did she ultimately achieve her goal. 'Well, there's one thing about this disease,' she said a few months before her death. 'It certainly makes you lose weight.' She still didn't fill in the graph – and of course neither did I. It was at about this time that Dod reached a new pinnacle of insensitivity when he and Zomp were discussing the recent death of a friend. Suddenly as though inspired he announced cheerily, 'She died of the same thing you have, dear.' His voice tailed off toward the end of the sentence but it was too late.

By now, old Thompson's health was declining. His wife, whom we'd only known as Mrs. Thompson, had died some years before and our handyman had become, as Dod put it, 'a bit strange,' and 'decidedly odd.'

Much against his will, he was put into a home but repeatedly absconded. Every few weeks he would leave the home and set off toward his old house and a few hours later the police would bring him back. Dod and I visited him once. It was a nice, clean, spacious home on the edge of Mousehold Heath and the staff seemed friendly. After exchanging greetings and reminding him who I was, I said to Thompson, 'What a nice place. You must be comfortable here.'

'It's awful! That man's trying to kill me,' he said, pointing towards an innocuous man in a wheel-chair, 'And they're all trying to poison me.'

Dod said diplomatically, 'I'm sure that's not the case, Mr Thompson.' Sadly, he could not be persuaded and continued to abscond until he died a few months later.

Zompie's health was now deteriorating quite rapidly. By this time, I had left home and Dod would occasionally telephone me to say that Zompie 'ponged a bit'. She refused to go into a hospice, however, and spent the last week of her life watching the World Snooker Championships on television with a vomit bowl in front of her. She died one evening while Dod and Woog were in the Constitution and they found her lying dead in the hall when they arrived back.

A few days later, friends and relatives gathered at No. 3 in the very place where she had died. We were having a pre-funeral drink while waiting for the hearse when Dod's brother, Ken, arrived. He had previously said that he would be unable to come, so it was a pleasant surprise when he walked through the front door and, after a brief greeting, said, 'I'd like a large whisky please – and then another one.'

Zompie's elder sister, Olive, became very tense and worried when the hearse was late in arriving. Looking at his watch Dod said loudly, 'Typical Zomp! Late for her own funeral,' I don't think anyone laughed at Dod's attempt at humour. The hearse eventually arrived and Dod, Woog and I followed it a sedate pace to St. Margaret's Church in Old Catton, where we sang the hymns that we'd chosen for the event. After the service, and with the coffin reinstated in the hearse, the cortège moved off slowly with the funeral director walking at its head. I was deeply moved to see him solemnly remove his black top hat and, holding it out at arm's length, bow his head and walk slowly in front of the hearse for the first fifty yards of the five mile journey to St Faith's crematorium. There, after a short service, Zompie's mortal remains disappeared from view for the last time.

CHAPTER 16: NORWICH HOTELS

After a spell working in London, Woog moved back to Norwich and, following a brief failed marriage, ended up living in College Road on the north side of the town. At that time I was living in Edinburgh so that visiting Norwich to see Dod and Woog was by no means straightforward. Dod by this time was in his seventies and living in a one-bedroom council flat, while Woog's house was a complete mess and his health so poor that I was not keen to take up the offer of staying with him.

I had nevertheless decided to take my partner, June, to Norwich to meet Dod and Woog. This was June's first visit to Norwich and it was now some thirty years since I had lived there. I could only remember the large expensive hotels and had no idea of smaller cheaper local accommodation, so phoned Dod to ask his advice,

'I would try the Heathcote Hotel,' he said. 'Your Aunt Edie used to stay there and she said it was very nice.'

Well, if it was good enough for Aunt Edie, who was well-known for her refined taste, it was good enough for me. Dod found me the phone number and I duly rang the hotel. After a lengthy wait, the phone was answered by a girl who asked in a young and timid voice, if she could be of help.

'Good evening,' I said. 'I was wondering if you had a double room for this weekend, Friday to Monday, and could you tell me how much that would cost?' There was silence and after a considerable pause came the hesitant reply, 'I'm not sure if we do that.'

I was slightly surprised by this response but, undeterred, went on: 'Would it be possible to find out, please?' She said she would enquire and, after another long delay, a second voice, male this time, came over the phone,

'Hello, how can I help you?'

I repeated my enquiry.

'I don't think we've ever been asked that before', came the reply. This seemed very strange, even for Norwich, where strange things do happen. I thought I would try once more.

'Is there any way you might be able to give me an indication if you have a double room for the weekend, and a rough idea how much it would cost?' I enquired politely.

'Well, we've asked everyone here and no one seems to know', and then after a pause he added, 'Sir'.

This again seemed decidedly odd but clearly I was getting nowhere so I thanked the man for his help and hung up.

We eventually found accommodation in the Cumberland Hotel on the south side of Norwich, convenient for Thorpe Station but about a three mile walk to north Norwich where both Dod and Woog lived. After settling in to the hotel, we walked to the Lily Langtry, a pub on Unthank Road, where June and I had arranged to meet Dod and Woog. After a pleasant stroll we were approaching the pub when June saw the sign.

'There it is,' she said. 'The Heathcote Hotel. That would have been much more convenient.' Having related my bizarre conversation to June on the way down from Edinburgh, I glanced over and sure enough there was a sign, partially obscured, with 'The Heathcote' boldly displayed. Interestingly, there was an ambulance parked outside, a long ramp up to the main entrance and about twenty zimmer frames neatly stacked nearby.

I looked up again, the sign near the entrance now being completely visible and proudly proclaiming; 'The Heathcote Residential Nursing Home' and then, in smaller print, 'Home for the Elderly and Infirm. Enquiries to. . .' followed by the telephone number that I had called.

I related this to Dod and Woog in the pub, pointing out to Dod that he'd tried to book us into a home for the elderly and infirm for the weekend. Neither of them seemed to realise the potentially serious consequences of his action and Dod reiterated,

'Well, your Aunt Edie liked it, but I suppose that was about forty years ago.'

As usual, we set off far too late for the restaurant, which was called the Red Rooster. What with lots of news to catch up on, and Dod's refusal to leave a pub on an uneven number of pints, it was about ten-thirty when we left the Lily Langtry to seek out the small, newly-opened Spanish restaurant where we had chosen to eat. It was a converted Edwardian corner shop, very cosy and very quiet. We were in fact the only customers there as it was just closing when we arrived. Dod, who didn't like eating what he referred to as 'foreign muck', found the menu a bit limited but calmed down when he realised he could have a steak. The rest of us being cosmopolitan types, who knew a thing or two about such foreign muck, shared tapas dishes. The food was good, we drank beer and wine; and after ice creams and cheese Dod decided we should have liqueurs and coffee. Dod ordered his favourite, Drambuie, and we drank and chatted. It was after midnight when I decided I should pay and then head for home.

I looked around for the waitress, a nice girl who was obviously a student earning a bit of money in her free time. She was sound asleep on her seat in a corner of the restaurant. It seemed a shame to wake her but I could hardly leave without paying. After some vigorous shaking she woke with a start and nearly fell off her chair. Once she had orientated herself and regained her composure, she apologised profusely and handed me the bill. I was astonished to discover that Dod had drunk 111 Drambuies, which was some going even for Dod. On my querying this, the waitress pointed out that the number in fact was three, which she had been written as three vertical lines. This came as a distinct relief to me, and also to Dod who could not remember drinking the other one hundred and eight.

It is an odd thing about old folk that they always claim to

have no appetite. This is blatantly untrue. On those visits to Norwich when we took Dod out for dinner he always said, 'Oh, I really couldn't eat a thing. I've no appetite at all nowadays,' and then would sit down and demolish a large plate of fish and chips, followed by ice cream. When asked about a pudding he'd remark, 'I might just manage a little cheese', adding, 'Well, yes, a Drambuie *would* be rather nice.' I would have hated to be paying the bill in the days when Dod had a good appetite.

On our next visit, the Cumberland Hotel was full but they advised us to try the Penrith. They had lots of free rooms there – not surprisingly as it turned out. While June was unpacking, I went to the bar to unwind over a beer or two after the tiring drive from Edinburgh. It has always been a problem for me that if there is someone in a bar who is a bit odd they always gravitate in my direction and start up a conversation. Maybe it's because I'm tall and easily noticeable, or have a kind face; or perhaps it's that I simply can't be rude to people and just tell them to bugger off. If there is an idiot in the bar, then nine times out of ten he will begin speaking to me. The tenth time is when I am quick enough to spot him first and leave by the back door.

On this occasion I wasn't quick enough and the man in question immediately started talking to me very loudly. I recognised the words but failed to understand the meaning, so nodded wisely whenever it seemed appropriate. At last June came to my rescue so that I could excuse myself and leave. Interestingly, I noticed that after I had left, he continued talking to the space where I had been, as though I was still there. This was rather peculiar – but (as you know) strange things do happen in Norwich and this could have been what is known as 'normal for Norfolk' where, because of its isolation, genes which have remained hidden for thousands of years are displayed openly.

The double bed was one of those U-shaped affairs where as a result of the basic laws of gravity the occupants each roll into the centre. This was not a good beginning and – allied to a little disturbance in the corridor in the middle of the night, which it is true could have happened in any hotel – we had a poor night's sleep. The Fort Knox-type locks on the bedroom door should also have given us a clue. At breakfast the next morning, we ordered the full English meal, which was glorious in its size and potential for inducing a coronary. It was then that June and I became aware of a conversation between a couple breakfasting at the next table. I think it was when one of them mentioned that their community psychiatric nurse was visiting them that day that it dawned on both of us simultaneously that this hotel was used as a half-way house for psychiatric patients who had been newly discharged from the secure unit of the local hospital. I vowed that on future trips I would pay extra and stay somewhere safe.

CHAPTER 17: DOD'S DEMISE

At some stage, one of Dod's dodgy business deals required a certain amount of capital investment and he re-mortgaged No. 3. This venture went the same way as all his other business projects and when Dod couldn't manage the payments the bailiffs were called in. After eviction Dod was initially housed in a B. and B. and a few months later in a one-bedroom council flat, No. 22 Causeway Close. When asked about this move, Dod said, 'The old house was getting too big for me,' implying that the move had been made by choice.

For a few more years he lived quite happily there, the routine of life interrupted only by regular visits from the Jehovah's Witnesses whose company he enjoyed; by a heart valve replacement, which he didn't particularly enjoy; by a prostate operation which was a great relief; and by a progressively worsening chest which limited his mobility significantly. He would still drive with complete disregard for the drink-driving laws. It is fair to say though that one New Year's Eve, while I was having a beer in his local with him, we were offered a free whisky. Asked if he wanted water in it, Dod answered after some hesitation, 'Yes, please, I might be driving later.' I didn't bother to point out to him the fundamental flaw in this thinking. Who knows? If he had lived long enough he might have got the hang of it.

After numerous close calls and admissions to hospital when somehow he stopped just short of the pearly gates, Dod collapsed at home and died soon after reaching hospital. The Woog was present and, perhaps surprisingly, Dod was heard to mutter the Lord's Prayer as he passed away.

The funeral was identical to Zomp's thirteen years before: identical, of course, apart from the identity of the deceased; the same church, St. Margaret's in Old Catton; the same lachrymose hymns, 'Abide with me ' and 'The Lord is my Shepherd'; the same crematorium and the same funeral directors. The vicar, however, was new. He said some nice things about Dod, and then came the procession to the crematorium.

Dod had always said that he didn't want a lot of flowers as they belonged in the garden, but that he would like a single red rose on his coffin. I had always remembered that and so duly put a single red rose along with the other flowers on the coffin as it lay in the back of the hearse. The funeral director asked if the flowers should be taken off the coffin or be cremated along with the body. It seemed appropriate for the flowers to be removed and recycled to some hospital ward or old folk's home. I said nothing about the rose, however, as it seemed rather picky and too much to ask for one particular flower to be left.

After the funeral service we drove to St Faith's and I sat with family members in the front row of the crematorium. As the coffin was solemnly shouldered past, I was amazed to see the single red rose perched rather precariously on the rear edge of the coffin. I watched it throughout the short service and at the end, as the coffin descended, the red rose was the last thing visible. Amazing that!

In fact, the first time June and I stayed at a 'proper' hotel in Norwich was on the occasion of Dod's funeral. I was fed up with staying in old folk's homes and psychiatric half-way houses, so when Dod's younger brother, my Uncle Ken, phoned to say that he'd be coming across from Wallasey with his partner, Adèle (assuming she'd recovered from her hip replacement by then) and asked if I would like him to book a room at the Beeches Hotel, where they were staying, I jumped at the offer. This seemed eminently sensible. I knew the Beeches well, since many years ago the father of one of my school friends had owned it. It definitely was not a residential home for the elderly, the mad or even the slightly disoriented, and we agreed that Ken should book rooms for all of us.

Sadly, once again things did not run as smoothly as we both would have wished, since two double rooms both in the name of Howard led to confusion. Ken had requested a ground floor room with easy access for Adèle and himself, as her mobility was still limited after the hip replacement and she still needed the aid of a zimmer frame. Ken and Adèle were therefore quite surprised when, on arrival they were directed to a first-floor room which could only be accessed by a tricky spiral staircase on which there were two small landings. This was difficult to negotiate if you were fully fit, and nigh on impossible with a zimmer. When asked, the receptionist said there was no other room available so, somehow or other Ken lifted, pushed and hoisted Adèle up the stairs to their room. June and I, on the other hand, were ushered into a ground floor room easily accessible from the front door. This confusion between the two Howards continued throughout the stay. When Uncle Ken treated us to dinner I found I was billed for it, but luckily when I reciprocated on another evening that meal went on Ken's bill.

* * *

A few weeks later Woog and I were clearing out Dod's flat. In the wardrobe we found his full evening dress, including a heavy white silk scarf, starched collars, a cartoon of himself in evening dress dated 1939, and Zompie's fur coat. On the doormat, along with the usual junk mail, was a letter from Norwich City Football Club. Woog opened it, drew out a brand new-five pound note and read, 'Dear Gold Bond Club Member. Congratulations, you have won a prize in the Gold Bond Draw'.

Woog and I laughed at the irony as we closed Dod's front door for the last time.